Essential Mysticism

by T.Collins Logan

Excerpts of "The Sky Gave Me Its Heart" and "First He Looked Confused" from *Love Poems from God* ©2002 Daniel Ladinsky, Penguin Group

Excerpt of "Someone Who Can Kiss God" from *I Heard God Laughing* ©1996 Daniel Ladinsky, Mobius Press

Excerpt of "Unmarked Boxes" from *The Essential Rumi* ©1995 Coleman Barks, HarperCollins

Everyday Zen, by Charlotte Joko Beck, HarperSanFrancisco 1989
The Path of Sufi Love by William C. Chittick, State University of NY 1983
The Way of Chuang Tzu by Thomas Merton, Hyperion 1994
Tales of the Hasim by Martin Buber, Schoken 1991
Anam Cara by John O'Donohue, HarperCollins 1998
Dream Conversations on Buddhism and Zen by Thomas Cleary, Shambhala 1996
The Bhagavad Gita translated by Eknath Easwaran, Nilgiri 1987
The Spiral Dance by Starhawk, HarperCollins 1989
Total Freedom by J. Krishnamurti, HarperSanFrancisco 1996
A Witches' Bible by Janet Farrar and Stewart Farrar, Phoenix 1996
The Mind of Light by Sri Aurobindo, Lotus 2004
Way of Zen by Martine Batchelor, Thorsons 2001
One Taste by Ken Wilber, Shambhala 2000
Will and Spirit by Gerald G. May, HarperCollins 1987
"The Guru and the Pandit," Andrew Cohen and Ken Wilber, www.wie.org
Miracluous Living by Shoni Labowitz, Fireside 1998
The Seven Spiritual Laws of Yoga by Deepak Chopra and David Simon, John Wiley & Sons, 2004
Passionate Presence by Catherine Ingram, Gotham 2004
"Our Ideal" by Sri Aurobindo, *Arya* 1914-1915
The Four Agreements by Don Miguel Ruiz, Amber-Allen 1997
The Eye Never Sleeps by Dennis Genpo Merzel, Shambhala 1991
Wandering on the Way by Victor H. Mair, University of Hawaii 1998

ESSENTIAL MYSTICISM, Third Edition, July, 2005.
Copyright ©2005 T.Collins Logan. All rights reserved.

ISBN 0-9770336-0-0

Excerpts from *The Vital Mystic, A Guide to Emotional Strength and Spiritual Enrichment* ©2003 T.Collins Logan

Cover design by Mollie Kellogg, www.molliekellogg.com
Editing services by Renata Golden, www.golden-ink.com

Published by Integral Lifework Center, PO Box 90936, San Diego, CA 92169

Printed in the United States of America

A special thanks to all my students.
Your questions, insights and sharing continue to inspire me.

Love and gratitude also to Mollie, who keeps encouraging me to teach.

Table of Contents

PREFACE   1

  Counting Breaths   3

1 – CULTIVATING A NEW WAY OF SEEING   5

  Transitions Through Gnosis   9
    Transporting Perceptions   10
    Merging of Self with Divine   10
    Dissolution of Self   10
  Different Perspectives on a New Way of Seeing   11
    Concept Affinity: Mystic Activation   13
  Sample Mystic Activators   14
    Gratitude Meditation   15
    Stimulating Intuition – Wandering   16
    Daily Reflections   16

2 – REFINING INTENTIONS   17

  Different Perspectives on Refining Intentions   20
    Concept Affinity: Disciplined Intention   21
  Sample Mystic Activators   22
    "Who Am I Right Now?" Self-Inquiry   22
    Stimulating Intuition – Inner Guide   23
    Daily Reflections   24

3 – TRANSFORMING IDENTITY   25

  Phases of the Mystic's Way   28
  Different Perspectives on Transforming Identity   29
    Concept Affinity: New Modes of Self   30
  Sample Mystic Activators   31
    Mantra Meditation – Part One   31
    Stimulating Intuition – Journaling   32
    Daily Reflections   32

4 – HARMONIZING ACTION AND INTENTION   33

    Culmination in a Peculiar Quality of Consciousness   35
    Risks and Benefits   37
  Different Perspectives on Action and Intention   38
    Concept Affinity: Artifacts of Will   40

Sample Mystic Activators	40
Mantra Meditation – Part Two (with Visualization)	40
Stimulating Intuition – Listening to Now	41
Daily Reflections	42
5 – APPLICATIONS AND CONSEQUENCES	**43**
Additional Mystic Activator Examples	43
Self-Care Meditation	44
First Invocation	46
Contemplating Presence and Absence	47
Returning to Emptiness	48
"Just for Today" Daily Reflections	49
Measuring Our Progress	51
The Contemplative-Emotive Learning Process	52
Spiritual Health of Emotional States	54
Stages of Being	55
The Nuances of Synchronicity	61
Self-Awareness, Self-Esteem and Self-Nourishment	62
The Cycle of Personal Growth	63
What Happens To Our Relationships?	64
Challenging Our Assumptions	65
Passive Assignment of Meaning	66
Active Assignment of Meaning	67
The Nature of Evil	67
Staying On Track	71
Enhancing Discernment	72
6 – THE PROMISE OF HUMAN POTENTIAL	**75**
Different Perspectives on Human Potential	77
Concept Affinity: Love-Consciousness	80
7 – RECURRING QUESTIONS	**81**
APPENDIX	**84**
The Pyramid of Self	84
Artifacts of Will	88
Mystic Activators Comparison	90
SUGGESTED READING	**91**

Integral Lifework

This book is an authorized component of Integral Lifework training

For more information visit www.integrallifework.com

Essential Mysticism

PREFACE

The substance of *Essential Mysticism* is derived from twenty years of interdisciplinary study and personal experience. In my own journey, mysticism has provided a wealth of purpose and meaning, explained mysterious events, and enabled a simple way of living in harmony with the Universe and myself. When I forget to practice, my life can quickly get out of balance. That is why sample exercises are included throughout this book, and why any intellectual grasp of mysticism is easily trumped by an experiential one. Since mysticism can be found in some form in nearly every spiritual tradition, the objective of this work is to present its essential elements rather than support a particular belief system. Readers will recognize concepts and approaches found in Sufism, Christian mysticism, Taoism, Vedanta and other systems of Yoga, Buddhism, Hermeticism, Wicca and other forms of Earth-centered spirituality, and Kabbalah. Within this rich tapestry, the common threads that unite and strengthen communities of faith shape the foundation of all mystical practice.

First written as a companion to my ongoing *Mysticism: Dialogue and Practice* courses, this is intended as a comprehensive introduction to mystical theory and application. It both borrows from and adds to my previous book, *The Vital Mystic*,[1] and patience and persistence with the tools provided here can accomplish many things. These include reliable access to ineffable experiences, personal inspiration and wisdom, maintaining physical health, and improving overall mental, emotional and spiritual well-being. How each of us experiences and interprets mystical events may be both private and unique, but the mystic's way is steadfastly universal in nature.

---

[1] A downloadable version is available at *www.searchforclarity.com*

Mystical principles and methods are likewise nonexclusive, benefiting practitioners of any faith tradition or none at all. A compelling aspect of the mystical approach is that it need not be spiritualized or even systemized, but offers intrinsic, practical value in each of its components. Mysticism also compliments any integral practice and enhances a broad spectrum of self-nourishing routines.

To begin, the *four core disciplines* of mysticism to be discussed are:

- Discipline of mind – cultivating a new way of seeing
- Discipline of heart – refining intentions
- Discipline of spirit – transforming identity
- Discipline of will – harmonizing action and intention in a new way of being

The concept of self-discipline is central to this book, mainly to provide supportive structures for radical leaps of consciousness. What begins as a small sacrifice of old habits enables a rejuvenation of personal possibility. As we free ourselves from willful certainties about what we know, we discover answers to enduring questions. What is the nature of our existence? What lies at the core of human identity? How can we remain conscious and compassionate in navigating choices in this ever-changing world? Does each of us have an individual purpose? Through mystical processes we encounter far-reaching answers and effective ways of living fully.

At the end of each of the core discipline chapters, you will find representative quotes from different belief systems, a comparison of terms used in different mystical traditions, and sample exercises to stimulate mystical awareness and intuitive perception. Following this, we will examine some specific applications of mystical principles, predictable consequences of those applications, and some significant milestones in personal evolution. The potential impact of the mystic's way on societal transformation is saved for last, but is certainly central to my own motivations for writing this book and teaching courses on mysticism. Just as there is no single path up the mountain of enlightenment, there is also no single, homogenous worldview promoted by mysticism. There are, however, many common values that are awakened and strengthened by mystic disciplines, and I hope you will find those reflected here.

Some additional topics covered include:

- The role of mystical practice in improving self-awareness, self-esteem and self-nourishment
- The contemplative-emotive model of personal development
- Rejuvenating our journey by continually questioning our beliefs, assumptions and values
- The influence of mysticism on our relationships and community
- A working definition of evil and how the mystic can respond to it
- How to exercise and strengthen discernment
- A consideration of "spiritual evolution" as humanity's greatest potential

At the end of the book you will find a list of questions to stimulate further exploration of the mystical experience. There is also an Appendix with tables and charts that illustrate central themes and comparative practices in many schools of mysticism. Just beneath the surface of our cursory thoughts and perceptions, there is a world of life-changing truths waiting to be discovered. Those who seriously engage the mystic's way will encounter this enduring reality, the Sacred in every moment, and profound and healing strengths within themselves.

Counting Breaths

In preparation for reading the first chapter, I encourage you to try the following exercise:

1. Find a quiet place where you can sit undisturbed for five to ten minutes. If possible, make it a private place where you won't be

tempted to feel self-conscious or be worried about falling asleep.
2. Sit with your hands cradled gently in your lap and your feet flat on the floor. Close your eyes and relax your body.
3. Breathe deeply into your belly through your nose. Many of us are used to breathing shallowly, only as far as our chest cavity, so it may be uncomfortable to stretch those lungs all the way down to your navel. But I encourage you to try it anyway.
4. After a few deep breaths, just breathe as you would normally.
5. Now begin to count your breaths: breathe in, breathe out, count one. Breathe in, breathe out, count two. Count up to five, then start over.

For someone who has never attempted an exercise like this, it can be challenging. Your thoughts may wander. You may think to yourself "This is silly!" and want to stop practicing and instead keep reading to uncover an explanation. But if you gently turn your attention back to counting breaths, and let those other thoughts, feelings and sensations float away, you will begin to nudge your consciousness in a new direction – a mystical direction. So even if you feel such an exercise might be pointless, give it a whirl before reading any further. One final note: several of my students report that rhythmic sounds (Shamanic drumming, a ticking clock, their own heartbeat) assist and support this approach to mental discipline. This may enhance your experience as well.

I – CULTIVATING A NEW WAY OF SEEING

Mysticism asserts that there is a seldom-used faculty available to all of us, one that some consider independent of our ordinary senses, emotions and rational thought. It is an expansive type of perception-cognition, evidenced in nearly every spiritual tradition, which provides holistic and dynamic insight into personal and universal truths. Sounds pretty heady, doesn't it? To further complicate things, because the information we receive through this faculty is often paradoxical, inexpressible, and inaccessible by any other means, it has sometimes been labeled esoteric, magickal or otherworldly. But it is nonetheless available to most everyone through conscious effort. Different belief systems describe this *mystical awareness* in different ways: "penetrating the veil of illusion," "experiencing an ultimate reality," "tasting the divine," "submerging ourselves in non-being," "wordless rapture," "entering perfect stillness," and so on. And although each of these could be a distinctly separate experience, our imperfect language has trouble nailing any of them down succinctly. So here I have grouped all types of mystical awareness under a broad umbrella of *spiritual cognizance* – perhaps because I tend to spiritualize the language of mysticism, but also because this type of perception-cognition has been fairly resistant to categorization.

There are a number of different methods to stimulate spiritual cognizance, each uniquely suited to diverse personalities, cultural values and life experiences. These *mystic activators* may fall into different categories, but all of them are designed with one end in mind: to suspend habitual thought processes – and the constant stream of input our physical senses provide – in order to induce a spiritually receptive being. Through modes of practice apposite to our personal tendencies and current phase of personal development, we can free our minds and hearts and nurture ourselves on many levels. Some mystic activators reform consciousness with rigorous concentration or repetition. Others are a deliberate supersaturation or overstimulation of our psyche to trigger alternative states that transcend self-absorption. Still other techniques gradually reduce or order the content of our thoughts and feelings until a quiescent stillness blossoms. All of these methods require explicit qualities of self-discipline and deliberate intention.

What awaits us at the end of these differing paths? A mystical union; a dissolving of Self in All; a vulnerable intimacy with the Sacred; a direct experience of infinite interconnectedness; a nondual consciousness we could call a *gnosis of the Absolute*. I use the term *gnosis* because I view this process as a sort of intuitive apprehension of All That Is, including nothingness. And although there are many intermediate experiences full of colorful and compelling content – many transitions into that ultimate intuition – the end state is completely empty of any constructs, differentiation, sensory input, emotional intensity or self-referential cognition. It is, rather, a state of awareness without an observer and without an object, while at the same time rich with meaning and import for our own well-being and the evolution of the Whole. In one way, it is a re-creation of the non-being from which all things originate, and from which we can create infinite possibilities. For me, gnosis has defined what it means to be "spiritual."

What about meditation? It is frequently a part of mystical practice, but it is a misunderstanding to equate the two. Meditation is one avenue of mental training, but what is so vitally important in all schools of mysticism is an ability to channel internal and external stimuli – however that can be achieved. If we are forever being overwhelmed by reactive emotions, by physical urges and appetites, by the obsessive cycling of our own thoughts, or by anything peripheral to inner quietude, we will have trouble remaining sensitive to subtler input. Being preoccupied with the random, we will seldom encounter our most extraordinary capacities and precious inner wisdom. Being attached to the illusion of our individuality and its sensorial experience of the moment, we will not experience the unity of All Things.

For most of us, our corporeal form, with all its complex chemistries and vast capacity for receiving and generating all kinds of information, tends to hold our immediate interest, always clamoring for our attention. And we often reinforce and amplify this clamoring by seeking to gratify our desires without a thought for the broader context of our existence or the meaning of our lives. Mystical practice is not about suppressing, coercing or forcing what is happening inside or outside, but it recognizes that we are the source of our own perception-cognition and of every want or whim that demands our consideration. We are a fount of endless desires. We can either shape this process actively or allow our environment and habitual propensities to shape it for us. Mysticism encourages us to remain perpetually conscious and awake, instead of relying on impulse, momentum or conditioning. The mystic's way consists of fully appreciating who we truly are, what we are doing here, and why we make the choices we make.

The following are the four main categories of mystic activators found among major mystical traditions.[2] Each approach tends to resonate with different people – or with the same person in different stages of being – and is often designed to support a particular underlying belief system.

- *Subtractive Meditation*

    Detaching from emotions, thoughts, and sensory experience in order to restructure consciousness and make room for mystical awareness. Often this is achieved through a systematic disassociation of subject and object – Self from other, mind from body, unconscious process from conscious process, being from doing, *this* from *that* – which sets our consciousness free. Sometimes, detachment is merely a byproduct of singular focus

---

[2] See **Mystic Activators Comparison** in the Appendix for specific examples

or a merging of subject and object. Expanded perception-cognition tends to be more incremental as a subtractive practice deepens, though epiphanies can also be surprisingly sudden.

- **Ecstatic Induction**

  Seeking to arouse a highly energized or blissful state that actuates mystical insight. This is frequently devotional in nature and usually employs physiological means of accelerating the letting go of habituated consciousness. Ecstatic induction can also result in what the ancient Greeks called *mania*, "possession by deity," a form of trance where self-awareness is greatly or entirely attenuated. Supersensory experiences tend to be more sudden and extreme than with other techniques.

- **Symbolic and Synchronistic Ritual**

  Procedures that are esoteric or symbolically abstracted, sometimes associated with devotional worship and sometimes not, which purposely invoke natural, energetic and/or spiritual forces. Mystical awareness can be an unintentional byproduct of these practices, or the goal. A key difference between this and other activators is that such rituals usually invite external agents or forces – which may or may not coincide with a particular quality of internal effort – to help generate transpersonal experience.

- **The Perfection of Love**

  A refinement and intensity of love that reforms our awareness. Once again, mystical perception-cognition is sometimes an intended goal, and sometimes a side effect of the central journey. The object and expression of love may vary: a deep compassion for the suffering of others; or fervent devotion to a transcendent presence; or intimate worship of deity. But the nearly universal outcomes are a surrendering of personal ego, new certainties and convictions (often imbued with a sense of holiness or awe), an aligning of personal will with the object of love, and a passionate desire to translate conviction into action. A transformative union with the Sacred, however that is defined by the tradition, is usually the primary objective of this path.

As varied as these methods – and our subjective perceptions of them – may be, they all attempt to cultivate the same result: a letting go of ordinary perception-cognition, and inviting an inner stillness that makes room for spiritual cognizance. A new way of seeing. Increasingly, my own mystic activator preference combines the perfection of love with subtractive meditation. However, I believe it is important to stimulate and nourish different aspects of Self through ongoing exploration, and I fully expect that, over time, other approaches will be better suited to different objectives or new phases of my growth. We must all find our own way. Examples of assorted mystic activators will follow each chapter, and a comparison chart of activators found among various traditions is available in the Appendix.

Transitions Through Gnosis

There is a commonly occurring sequence of sudden shifts in awareness brought about by mystical practice. These *transitions through gnosis* have three distinct traits, which are perhaps the primary features of all spiritual cognizance: a riveting absorption in, and appreciation of, the present moment; increasing clarity about personal purpose and universal truths; and a radical departure from previous understanding. A predictable progression of these transitions suggests a peeling away of abstractions and a gradual freeing of the mind from its attachment to aesthetic and reasonable appearances – especially regarding what initially seems to be incredible or incomprehensible data. At first we might encounter the mystical through emotions, as imagery, or even as physical sensations. But eventually we experience an unmediated contact that reforms all of our previous constructs or removes them altogether. This progression is not rigid, and we should be careful not to evaluate the quality of our mystical awareness as an indication of spiritual achievement. In fact, the more sincere our effort, the less meaning all comparison will hold for us. Nevertheless, unless our practice culminates in a gnosis of the Absolute, we have not reached even the beginning of the end of our mystical journey.

Here are some of the transitions through gnosis commonly experienced by mystics of many different traditions:

Transporting Perceptions

- Journeying outside of the body in the physical realm or to other planes of existence
- Communicating directly with other spiritual intelligences
- Prophetic visions, inspirational voices, automatic writing, or other forms of revelatory knowledge

Merging of Self with Divine

- Complete openness and seamless union with a Sacred Presence or Vital Continuum, often coinciding with a fathomless embrace of transcendent love
- Pervasive joy beyond comprehension; a bliss exceeding our capacity to contain it; an awakening of *agape* love-consciousness, where unconditional adoration and compassion for All Things consumes our being and directs our will
- Direct, unmitigated contact with the Divine Spark within us – our transcendent nature, our True Self

Dissolution of Self

- Infinite awareness, expanding inward and outward, incomprehensibly encompassing all time and space, transfixed by a unity of existence that has no discrete components or differentiating characteristics
- An awe-inspiring – and sometimes terrifying – submersion in emptiness, nothingness, or a state of unknowing free of all concepts, emotions or sensations, and ultimately devoid of any self-conscious awareness
- A complete, unconditional surrender of Self to these unitive states

If we remain watchful, mindful and aware, diligently applying all that we learn through mystical practice with intentions informed by a broader purpose, we will eventually arrive at a holistic gnosis of raw, unadorned reality and all its numinous truths. Then the most dramatic transformations can begin, with irrefutable benefits to ourselves and the world in which we live. If we resist applying what we come to know, or otherwise avoid accountability to our newly discovered inner Light, our mystical journey will be of little benefit to anyone and we will become forgetful tourists in the land of Self. So both intentionality and follow-through are crucial to viable mysticism. But what might "spiritually profitable intentions" look like? And what is a proposed broader purpose for the mystic? That is what we will discuss in the following chapter.

Different Perspectives on a New Way of Seeing

At the end of each of the first four chapters, I have included mystical writings that relate to that chapter's themes. You may find them useful in enlarging or reinforcing your conception of mystical experience and practice, and I encourage you to examine the source material for further insights into the spiritual traditions from which they arose. Compare them, meditate on them, and see if you can catch a glimpse of the common ground they share. Please note that I have included the translators in parenthesis wherever possible.

"For to understand is to believe, but not to believe is not to understand. My speech or words do not reach the Truth, but the mind is great, and being guided for a while by speech, it is eventually able to attain the Truth."
– *Corpus Hermeticum*

"The perception of the divine omnipresence is essentially a seeing, a taste, that is to say a sort of intuition bearing upon certain superior qualities in things. It cannot, therefore, be attained directly by any process of reasoning, nor by any human artifice."
– Teilhard de Chardin

"For some people, depending on their personal conditioning and history, this process may go smoothly, and the release is slow. For others, it comes in waves, enormous emotional waves. It's like a dam that bursts. We fear being flooded and overwhelmed. It's as though we've walled off part of the ocean, and when the dam breaks the water just rejoins that which it truly is; and it's relieved because now it can flow with the current and the vastness of the ocean."

– Charlotte Joko Beck

"Intellect is good and desirable to the extent it brings you to the King's door. Once you have reached His door, then divorce the intellect...You have no business with the how and wherefore. Know that the intellect's cleverness all belongs to the vestibule. Even if it possesses the knowledge of Plato, it is still outside the palace."

– Jelaluddin Rumi (William C. Chittick)

"The hearing of the spirit is not limited to any one faculty, to the ear, or to the mind. Hence it demands the emptiness of all the faculties. And when the faculties are empty, then the whole being listens. Then there is a direct grasp of what is right there before you that can never be heard with the ear or understood with the mind."

– Chuang Tzu (Thomas Merton)

"One day it dawned on me that man cannot attain to perfection by learning alone. I understood what is told of our father Abraham; that he explored the sun, the moon, and the stars, and did not find God, and how, in this very not-finding, the presence of God was revealed to him. For three months I mulled over this realization. Then I explored until I too reached the truth of not-finding."

– Yaakov Yitzhak of Pzhysha (Martin Buber)

"Self-knowledge is not gained by explanations and descriptions, or by the instructions of others. At all times, everything is known only through direct experience."

– Vasishtha (Swami Venkatesananda)

"The first step in awakening to your inner life and to the depth and promise of your solitude would be to consider yourself for a little while as a stranger to your own deepest depths. To decide to view yourself as a complete stranger, someone who has just stepped ashore in your life, is a liberating exercise. This meditation helps break the numbing stranglehold of complacency and familiarity. Gradually, you begin to sense the mystery and magic of yourself."

– John O'Donohue

Concept Affinity: Mystic Activation

As part of evaluating different perspectives, I am also including specific terms from a small sampling of spiritual traditions. It is important to remember that many of these terms have multiple or layered meanings, often within the same tradition and nearly always when similar words are used in different traditions. In most instances the spelling supplied here is the more common English rendering; in the case of Chinese characters I provide pinyin and some alternate spellings. For additional examples and clarification, a regularly updated version of this chart including foreign language characters is available at www.searchforclarity.com.

How we understand new concepts is less about concise definitions and more about the vocabulary of our personal experience and our current state of mind. In researching ideas from different mystical systems that have similar qualities, themes or overlapping functions, I encourage you to come to your own conclusions. Is the mystical process universal? Do the same underlying structures support what seem on the surface to be competing concepts? Only life-long immersion in a given practice can reveal the subtle nuances of system-specific language, and we must be careful to avoid homogenizing or haphazardly syncretizing. But as we continue to explore these ideas, they can help us interpret our own ineffable experiences and better harness a distinctly mystical flavor of knowledge.

What follow, then, are examples of mystic activators and their approximate transitions through gnosis within each tradition.

Essential Mysticism

Zen Buddhism	Christian Mysticism	Kabbalah	Sufism	Taoism	Kundalini Yoga
Shikantaza	Contemplative Prayer (Theoria/ Contemplatio)	Hitbonenut	Dhikr ↓ Mushahada	Microcosmic Orbit (Hsiao Chou Tien)	Kriyas (Mudras & Bandhas) ↓ Dharana
Joriki	Kenosis	Chochmah Binah Da'at (Yichuda Tata'Ah)	Fana'	Xīn Zhāi	Dhyana
Kensho ↓ Satori	Illumination & Gnosis Kardias (Gnosis)		Ma'rifa ↓ 'Irfan	(Kuan) Guān ↓ Shén Míng	Aparoksha Anubhuti
Nirodha	Cloud of Unknowing (Apophatic)	Ayin (Bitul)	Fana' al-Fana'	Wú	Shunyata
Nirvana	Unio Mystica (Henosis)	Devekut (Yichuda ila'Ah)	'Ayn al-Jam	(Tao) Dào	Parashakti (Savikalpa Samadhi)
	Unmanifest Godhead	Ein Soph	Wara u'l-Wara		Nirguna Brahman (Nirvikalpa Samadhi)

Sample Mystic Activators

And now some simple – but not so simple – practice activators. If you haven't already tried the "counting breaths" exercise at the end of the Preface, I suggest working with that first to strengthen your concentration. Also, you can always return to counting your breaths if you find yourself getting lost in any of the more complex activators.

Gratitude Meditation

1. Objective: Between 15 and 75 minutes of continuous meditation each day. If you can, insulate this with a buffer of five minutes before and after so it never feels rushed, and so you have time to reflect on your experiences.
2. Find a quiet place to sit and relax, and begin your meditation with an inner commitment to a broader goal than just personal edification, i.e. "May this be for the good of All."
3. Relax every part of your body. Start with your hands and feet – perhaps moving them or shaking them a little to release tension – then your arms and legs, then your torso, head and neck.
4. Breathe deeply and evenly into your stomach, preferably in through the nose and out through the mouth, so that your shoulders remain still but your stomach "inflates." Practice this until you are comfortable with it.
5. In the middle of your chest, just above and behind your sternum, gradually fill your heart with gratitude. It need not be directed at anything or anyone, but you could shape this as an offering to the Source of Life, or Nature, or deity, or simply to the present moment.
6. Begin with a small point of feeling, and allow it to slowly spread with each breath until it fills your whole being. For some, it may be helpful to visualize this spreading gratitude as light emanating from a point in the center of the chest. Maintain this state for as long as you can.
7. As other images, sensations, feelings, or thoughts arise, let them go and return to your offering of gratitude.
8. If you become disquieted, uncomfortable, jittery, or severely disoriented, try to relax through it. If the sensations persist or become extreme, cease all meditation for the day.
9. Give yourself space after your meditation to process what you have experienced. Just *be* with what has happened without judgment or a sense of conclusion.

For some, this exercise will be easy. For others, nigh unto impossible. Don't worry – both success and failure are meaningless. Neither proves anything, or guarantees or denies eventual gnosis of the Absolute. Remember that, especially in the beginning, practice is more about learning to let go of old habits than creating special consciousness. Epiphanies can't be forced, but we can eventually condition our mind, heart and spirit to become more inviting for them.

Stimulating Intuition – Wandering

Along similar lines of experimentation, also try the following exercise to stimulate your intuition.

Go for a walk in a place unfamiliar to you, without a clear destination or time limit. Begin by deciding which way to go – left, right or straight – without a logical or a deliberate objective. Instead, try to feel your way through each change in direction, noting the sensations in your solar plexus or middle diaphragm as you consider which way to go. Do you feel a lifting, freeing sensation for one option? Try going in that direction. Do you feel a clenching sensation? Try avoiding that direction. See what happens. At some point you may lose your sense of place and time altogether – that's great! If this happens, can you follow your internal promptings back to where you began...?

Daily Reflections

Another approach to interior discipline is to reflect in a structured way on concepts that that commonly fall within mystical experience, or that frequently surface in mystical writings. To this end, I have provided a list of daily reflections on pages 49-50. Because these can accompany other activities, they may be a helpful starting point for some. Pick two or three at random that appeal to you, copy them down to take with you, and try the "Just for Today" reflective practice on for size. Throughout the day, speak them aloud or silently as questions, as affirmations, as declarations. Apply them thoughtfully to your interactions and your responses in each new situation. Try to feel each of them in your heart as a hope, as a desire, as a belief, and as an acceptance of what already is.

2 - REFINING INTENTIONS

I cannot emphasize enough that actuating spiritual cognizance and encountering a gnosis of the Absolute without concurrently developing the most beneficial of intentions can have counterproductive, sometimes even disastrous consequences. Questing after knowledge, trying to find inner peace, gaining personal power or becoming a more compassionate agent of positive change are all inadequate motivations. In mysticism such desires, however impassioned, must be subordinated to an overarching intention to align oneself with the "good of All," even if we are not certain how that is defined. Mainly, this is so we become less attached to personal enrichment and our own interpretations of right and wrong, and more attentive to an all-inclusive developmental process. Even if we suspect the good of All is inevitable, or is destined to advance without our personal contributions, couldn't we still enhance it through the focus of our consciousness and will? The orientation that we can – and the conviction that we must – is called the *golden intention*.

What is the good of All, then? In short, I believe it is the spiritual evolution of the Universe itself. But what I believe is irrelevant, and you should discover any shared understanding through your own mystical journey. The key is trusting that the good of All is possible, and that we can in fact bind ourselves to it. We may never grasp the entire picture as it relates to our current actions – though spiritual cognizance will of course help us in this regard – but if we discipline our hearts to sincerely desire what is best for All Things, including ourselves, then it does not matter if we are certain of any specific direction or outcome. In fact, mysticism tends to discard moralizing and determinacy in favor of personal integrity with a simple principle: to develop as our first priority the habit of acquiescing to a higher nature, and thereby enter a flow of personal directedness supported by the Universe itself. In a way this is an article of faith, but it is a necessary one evident in all branches of mysticism, and it grounds our spiritual practice.

As to what the golden intention looks like for us individually, that is also for each of us to discover. However, there is more agreement than disagreement among mystical teachings about some of its critical features. These include:

- A letting go of ego, our compulsion to control externals, and any attachment to outcomes

- A sincere and generous wish for the well-being of others, with all our wants either inspired or managed by unconditional love-consciousness

- A passion for spiritual truth that is equally generous, unassuming, and ego-free; a heart that humbly thirsts to know why we are here and then act in accord with that purpose

- Persisting gratitude and celebration in every situation

The ego focuses our will on our most inconsequential desires, forever striving to hold onto whatever seems to have the highest immediate attraction, but which often has the lowest long-term value. The golden intention trains us to free ourselves from ego. When we are perpetually filled to overflowing with thankfulness and loving kindness, diligently centered on the well-being of others and the positive evolution of the Whole (remembering that all actions should coincide with our own nourishment and peace), we will always be acting from a place of efficacy and noble purpose. Thus we ultimately come to experience the harmony of Self-in-All and are completely fulfilled. This does not mean the intended consequences of our actions are guaranteed, or that we should not try to be wise and discerning in our choices, but it can be reliably observed that having such clear and sincere intentions integrates us into the unstoppable forces of good in the Universe.

Once again, this is about replacing unconscious and externally conditioned habits with consciously generated patterns. But here, instead of restructuring mental or perceptual processes with the objective of mystical awareness, we are changing our motivational orientation to the world around us. The I/me/mine fixation of childish egocentrism is relinquished in favor of selflessness, continually and dynamically redefined according to new mystical information. Through mystic activation, this information is personal, private and as perfectly suited to our current stage of being as it is Universal in nature. As we look within, the world without clarifies itself.

What are the negative consequences of not refining our intentions? At the least, we will certainly inhibit our own evolution, wellness, and happiness. At the worst we may cripple or injure ourselves, inadvertently antagonize the well-being of others, or even reinforce influences in the world that are disruptive to the progress of the Whole. It is not at all wise to activate the mystical without the golden intention. How could we handle an encounter with the Infinite without first refocusing our hearts? It would be like a person of average means being given unlimited funds without any explanation or a plan to manage such wealth. At first it might seem exciting and freeing, but it would quickly become a burden and a stress, and ultimately induce either self-destructive arrogance or angst. With the humility inherent to the golden intention, there is little opportunity for prideful self-deceit, and with the good of All informing every action and reaction, there is no room for distress or despair, but only compassionate conviction and joyful contentment that surpass all understanding.

This is likely the reason why most spiritual traditions encourage retraining the heart as part of their central disciplines. An advantage for the mystic is that daily emersion in spiritual cognizance naturally reinforces a compassionate worldview. Still, the farther I travel into the mystic's realm, the more I must remind myself what is important, and set aside childish impulses to gratify desires without the good of All in mind.

Different Perspectives on Refining Intentions

"The heart is a vessel that cannot remain empty. As soon as you have emptied it of all those transitory things you loved so inordinately, it is filled...with gentle heavenly divine love that brings you to the water of grace."
– St. Catherine of Siena

"People sometimes go mad from doing Zen meditation. This may happen when some perception or understanding arises through meditation, and the practitioner becomes conceited about it. It may also happen when the practitioner has unsolved psychological problems. Then again, it can happen through excessive physical and mental strain due to greedy haste to attain enlightenment."
– Muso Kokushi (Thomas Cleary)

"A person who has given up all desires for sense gratification, who lives free from desires, who has given up all sense of ownership and is devoid of false ego...only this person can attain lasting peace."
– *Bhagavad Gita* (Eknath Easwaran)

"The sky gave me its heart because it knew mine was not large enough to care for the earth the way it did."
– Rabia (Daniel Ladinsky)

"The mind is seeking security, permanency; it is moved by a desire to be safe, and can such a mind be free to find out what is true? To find out what is true, must not the mind let go of its beliefs, put away its desire to be secure?"
– J. Krishnamurti

"People waste energy defining which state they are in, as if consciousness were a cosmic grammar school in which third-graders were entitled to look down on kindergartners. The point is not what level we are on, but what we are learning."

– Starhawk

"For those who have not experienced this, consider our earthly longings and the joy of winning what we most desire. Remember that the objects of that earthly love are perishable and injurious – it is a love of imitations. It goes awry because we were mistaken; our good wasn't here and this wasn't what we truly sought. But Beyond is the true object of our love, where we can hold it and be with it and truly possess it, because we are no longer separated from it by flesh...."

– Plotinus

"I am always fearful of being more clever than devout. I would rather be devout than clever, but more than both devout and clever, I would like to be good."

– Rabbi Pinhas

"Oh Great Spirit...Make my hands respect the things You have made, my ears sharp to hear Your voice. Make me wise so that I may know the things You have taught my people, the lesson You have hidden in every leaf and rock. I seek strength not to be greater than my brother, but to fight my greatest enemy, myself."

– Chief Yellow Lark

Concept Affinity: Disciplined Intention

Zen Buddhism	Christian Mysticism	Kabbalah	Sufism	Taoism	Kundalini Yoga
Samma Sankappa	Mimesis	Kavannah	Muraquba	Wú Wéi	Vairagya

Sample Mystic Activators

Here are additional sample activators that may resonate more with one person than another. Try them once a day for a few weeks and see what works for you.

"Who Am I Right Now?" Self-Inquiry

1. Objective: Between 15 and 75 minutes of continuous meditation each day. If you can, insulate this with a buffer of five minutes before and after so it never feels rushed, and so you have time to reflect on your experiences.
2. Find a quiet place to sit and relax, and begin your meditation with an inner commitment to the golden intention, i.e. "May this be for the good of All."
3. Relax every part of your body. Start with your hands and feet – perhaps moving them or shaking them a little to release tension – then your arms and legs, then your torso, head and neck.
4. Breathe deeply and evenly into your stomach, preferably in through the nose and out through the mouth, so that your shoulders remain still but your stomach "inflates." Practice this until you are comfortable with it.
5. With your mind's eye centered in the middle of your chest, just above and behind your sternum, silently ask yourself "Who *am* I right now?" As words, images, feelings or experiences arise within you, create space for them in your mind and heart without judgment or analysis, and just rest in them for a moment. What arises may reflect the past, the present, or a desired future. If nothing happens at first, simply keep breathing and ask again, perhaps changing the emphasis on each word, as in: "*Who* am *I* right now?"
6. After you have rested in each event a while, let it go. That is, release any attachment or certainty you might have about these private thoughts, and gently set them aside. Avoid forcibly rejecting or denying what you find, but allow it to be deliberately tenuous, questionable, optional. You might resist wanting to let go of what you find. Nevertheless, it is important to release all that you encounter – try breathing it out with your

exhale. Comfortable in your uncertainty, enlarge the question by emphasizing other words, such as: "Who am I *right now?*"

7. Repeat the cycle of questioning, acknowledging without judgment, and letting go. If anything resurfaces repeatedly, try confronting it by asking "Why?" Rest in the response you receive to this question just as you rested in your previous inquiry, and then let that go as well. Continue questioning with new emphasis: "*Who am I* right now?"

8. If you become disquieted, uncomfortable, jittery, or severely disoriented, try to relax through it. If uncomfortable sensations persist or become extreme, cease all meditation for the day.

9. Give yourself space after your meditation to process what you have experienced. Just *be* with what has happened without judgment or a sense of conclusion.

Stimulating Intuition – Inner Guide

In a quiet place, visualize an imaginary person in your mind. Be as detailed as possible with your visualization of them – their features, their clothing, the place where they are, any activities they are doing, and so on. Get comfortable with this image until it seems to have a life of its own. Now imagine this person pausing in their activities, turning towards you and speaking to you. There doesn't have to be specific topic of conversation, just let them speak or remain silent, as they will. Notice all the emotions you are feeling. Notice how the person looks at you and interacts with you. If they speak, can you understand what they are saying? Do they even speak your language? Or do you perhaps understand the meaning they seem to be conveying, regardless? If you sense a connection or an ability to communicate, try asking this person a question and carefully consider their answer. If some pressing issue is on your mind, ask them for advice. Try to receive their response with openness and optimism. Then thank them for their time and reflect on your experience.

Daily Reflections

Consider copying or memorizing a new set of two or three Just for Today reflections from the list on pages 49-50. This time, however, choose some that either don't make immediate sense to you, or which you perhaps find difficult to accept on some level. By strengthening our relationship with concepts that challenge habitual thinking, we can stretch and reshape our awareness in ways that welcome spiritual cognizance. Let each idea fill you up – as a sound, as a color of light, as a sensation of warmth. Flood your body, mind and spirit with new possibilities.s

3 - TRANSFORMING IDENTITY

Once we have begun to discipline our mind and set our consciousness free, while at the same time redirecting the inclinations of our heart, a change occurs in how we view the Universe, other people and ourselves. Initially, this process will challenge many of the underlying beliefs, values and assumptions we have accumulated during our lives. It will also introduce new elements into our character, begin to alter priorities in our day-to-day existence, and augment many of our overall life goals with additional purpose. What eventually occurs over the course of ongoing practice is a synthesis – or perhaps more accurately an unveiling – of a completely new identity.

What is this identity? In the most general sense, it reflects the height of mystical experience itself: a dissolution of the individual in the All, a surrender of personal ego into deepest connection with an underlying reality. Here we let go of the various personas we have constructed since childhood – external masks of Self we have used to interact with the world – so that we rest easily in our True Self, that kernel of being we might call a soul or Divine Spark. From one perspective, we align our spirit with the Spirit of All; from another, the unitive spirit possesses us completely. And so we identify Self with the Whole, aborting any defense of personal distinctiveness, to navigate an integral perception of each moment from a persistently nondual consciousness. There is neither *this*, nor *that*, but only undifferentiated unity. But what distinguishes this transformation of identity from the mystical merging we have experienced through progressive awakenings? We now entirely embrace and become what we encountered during those peak moments. We occupy and express a gnosis of the Absolute with every breath, interacting with all things from an authentic center – rather than from a distant, irregular orbit around that center. First we come to know our own soul; then we learn to dwell in it and illuminate our way with its magnificent Light.

Of course, this kind of transcendental, transpersonal self-realization is not necessarily easy to achieve or endure. Facing the Infinite can be disorienting. Releasing our previous sense of Self can be frightening. Exposing every corner of our consciousness to utter emptiness is far easier to ignore or reject than to joyfully embrace. Nor is any of this an all-or-nothing proposition, as there are both intermediate stages of a Universe-inclusive Self and the natural ebb and flow of our mystic discipline. In the *Vital Mystic*, I describe this as a physiological/experiential/spiritual balancing act,[3] where at any given time one part of our makeup may dominate our being. Over time, we can learn to relax into a unified state and an existence that harmonizes everything within and without. So wherever we are in this process, our identity is subject to constant renewal. We can direct that renewal purposely, or risk having it tossed about on the ocean of experience without a clear idea of what we are doing here.

Another way to describe this re-identification process is as a successive death and rebirth of Self. This ongoing series of personal losses and recoveries is not just a figurative explanation of personal evolution, but a very real and sometimes painful freeing from previous identities, assumptions and modes of operation. For the mystic this is also not something that merely happens to us; we are not passive receptors of life-changing experience, but willing and rigorously self-aware participants. Even so, there can still be grief over sacrificing familiar self-justifications and coping mechanisms, and to whatever extent we hold onto that grief or resist accepting our new liberty and power, the more we will suffer even as we grow.

---

[3] See **Pyramid of Self** in the Appendix

Each loss builds on the foundation of previous stages of development, supporting the next layer of Self through new means of perception, motivation and self-reliance. With every mystical resurrection, we liberate ourselves from attachments and dependencies that have previously dictated our life's course and purpose. At first we might let go of animalistic impulses and purely emotional reasoning; then rationalist rigidity and experiential conditioning; then the limitations of past intuitions and epiphanies; and ever onward. Ultimately, we will even relinquish any attachment to nondual consciousness and a gnosis of the Absolute. In fact, nearly everything that we once considered a worthwhile goal or endpoint for our journey will become just another bend in the road, a false peak in our hike up the mountain of self-realization.

Not surprisingly, as we start activating mystical perception-cognition, this progress is echoed in transitions through gnosis. Our expanding awareness keeps introducing us to a potential "next self," so that we can begin weighing the costs and benefits of each transition before actually committing to change. Our successive *stages of being*[4] also parallel this course. Increasingly, we encounter patterns of continuous emancipation and reinvention nearly everywhere while engaging our surroundings with a mystical eye. The chart on the following page attempts to capture some of these correlations as they relate to common phases of the mystic's way.

But what does all this mean? It means we are not selfish anymore. It means we have shifted the central reference of our consciousness away from I/me/mine to the Whole of Creation. It means we no longer crave control over external situations or the fulfillment of any want, because we inhabit the essence of everything we ever *could* want. It means we are deeply in love with the All, even as we cease discriminating our Self from that All. It means we have let go entirely, and thus serendipitously come to possess the only thing worth having. It means we embody peaceful equilibrium, directedness, joy, perfected intention, and the power of transformation in an entirely new way of being. And then…our comprehension is enlarged once more. Growth never ends.

---

[4] See pages 55-61 in the Applications and Consequences chapter

Phases of the Mystic's Way

Pyramid of Self	Stages of Being	Correlating Phases of a Mystical Journey
Physiological Animal, Emotional & Rational	Stages 1-2	Initial suspicion of there being "more than meets the eye" about our existence. Curiosity, often characterized as spiritual thirst, leading to the first exploration and insight into transcendent experience.
Experiential Instinctive, Sagacious & Intuitive	Stages 3-4	First momentous encounter with spiritual forces, other realms of existence, or the wisdom of our own soul, and a resulting "awakening" to – or confirmation of – an awe-inspiring vastness beyond comprehension. For some the Divine, for others the Eternal, the Infinite or the Void. After some initial doubt and resistance, our "thirst" deepens.
	Stages 5-7	An adoption of personal discipline to further develop sensitivity to, and application of, spiritual cognizance in day-to-day life. This almost always manifests as improved management of emotions (relinquishing fears and compulsions, for example), freeing ourselves from attachments, desires and expectations, and expanding and sharpening our watchfulness – our "contemplative attention." Like any birthing process, however, there can be considerable emotional and existential distress involved as we leave our "pre-integrated Self" behind.
Spiritual Shared Understanding, Moments of Epiphany & Mystical Awareness	Stages 8-9	The first fruits of disciplined effort: a noticeable improvement in self-awareness; greatly clarified thought; a better understanding of spiritually healthy objectives and processes; overall humility; and increasing ease and congruity to all choices. A more transparent access to intuition and the shared understanding of the Universe, and progressively deepening epiphanies or "moments of awakening."
	Stages 10-11	An unconditional commitment to love: that is, compassion without boundaries or expectations; a true blossoming of *agape* love-consciousness from the soul. Perfection of the golden intention and freedom from ego. A resulting fluidity of action and positive outcomes, and continued strengthening of wisdom. This is often the natural segue to exploring more advanced mystical practices (see *Mystic Activators*).
	Stage 12	A surprisingly easy letting-go of Selfhood. Ongoing exploration of an ever-changing mystical horizon. The first taste of true spiritual freedom (from confining concepts, attachments and desires). A profound understanding that surpasses words or ideas; a spiritual knowledge dwarfing intellectual apprehension. A gnosis of the Absolute, resulting in a complete reorganization of reality and a whole new orientation of consciousness. A glimpse of the harmonized existence that results from persistent mystical practice.
	Stage 13	The continually expanding consequences of living in harmonized existence with our spiritual nature, gnosis of the Absolute, and the Source of Life at all times. Among these are a more spacious comprehension and actuation of *agape* from moment to moment, reinforced clarity of purpose, a profound sense of tranquility that subordinates all concerns, and a greatly simplified life-approach.
Divine Spark or "True Self"	Stage 14	Dissolving into the Divine Spark, the Sacred Center of our soul, where we no longer sense, or feel, or know, but are forever *being and becoming*. This is truly beyond words, but could be described as: "entering into the ultimate reality behind all that is," or "letting go of all concepts and differentiation to inhabit the essence of what remains."

T.Collins Logan

Different Perspectives on Transforming Identity

"I came to realize that mind is no other than mountains and rivers and the great wide earth, the sun and the moon and the stars."

— Dogen

"And thou who thinkest to seek for me, know thy seeking and yearning shall not avail thee unless thou knowest the mystery: that if that which thou seekest thou findest not within thee, then thou wilt never find it without thee. For behold, I have been with thee from the beginning; and I am that which is attained at the end of desire."

— *A Witches' Bible*

"Life evolves out of Matter, Mind out of Life, because they are already involved there: Matter is a form of veiled Life, Life a form of veiled Mind. May not Mind be a form and veil of a higher power, the Spirit, which would be supramental in its nature? Man's highest aspiration would then only indicate the gradual unveiling of the Spirit within, the preparation of a higher life upon earth...."

— Sri Aurobindo

"*That a quest there is, and an end, is the single secret spoken.* Under one symbol or another, the need of that long slow process of transcendence, of character building, whereby she is to attain freedom, become capable of living upon high levels of reality, is present in her consciousness. Those in whom this growth is not set going are no mystics...however great their temporary illumination may have been."

— Evelyn Underhill

"Unless a grain of wheat falls into the earth and dies, it remains by itself alone. But if it dies, it bears much fruit."

— *Gospel of John*

"We realize that nothing belongs to us truly, we can only care for it while it lasts. We also experience that we do not have a solid, separate identity. We are a flow of conditions. We are made up of all our genes, history, social conditioning, etc. Who are we but a bundle of aggregates and fluctuations? We cannot identify with our feelings, our thoughts, our possessions. They all come and go. They rise upon certain circumstances, stay a while and disappear."

– Martine Batchelor

"Meditation speeds up evolution. It accelerates the remembering and the re-discovery of the Spirit that you eternally are. Meditation quickens the rate that acorns grow into oaks, that humans grow into God."

– Ken Wilber

"You are never alone because you are full of memories, all the conditioning, all the mutterings of yesterday; your mind is never clear of all the rubbish it has accumulated. To be alone you must die to the past....In this solitude you will begin to understand the necessity of living with yourself as you are, not as you think you should be or as you have been."

– J. Krishnamurti

"I could not lie anymore so I started to call my dog 'God.' First he looked confused, then he started smiling, then he even danced. I kept at it: now he doesn't even bite. I am wondering if this might work on people?"

– Tukaram (Daniel Ladinsky)

Concept Affinity: New Modes of Self

Zen Buddhism	Christian Mysticism	Kabbalah	Sufism	Taoism	Kundalini Yoga
Mujodo No Taigen	Theosis & Fruit of the Spirit	Netzach Hod Yesod	Baqa' bi Allah	Wú Wéi	Svadharma
Bodhisattva	Sainthood	Tzaddik	Awliya' Allah	Shèng Rén	Purna Yogi

Sample Mystic Activators

Mantra Meditation – Part One

1. Objective: Between 15 and 75 minutes of continuous meditation each day. If you can, insulate this with a buffer of five minutes before and after.
2. Find a quiet place to sit and relax, and begin your meditation with an inner commitment to the golden intention, i.e. "May this be for the good of All."
3. Relax every part of your body. Start with your hands and feet – perhaps moving them or shaking them a little to release tension – then your arms and legs, then your torso, head and neck.
4. Breathe deeply and evenly into your stomach, preferably through the nose, so that your shoulders remain still but your stomach "inflates." Practice this until you are comfortable with it.
5. Begin the "four-fold" breath – that is: breathe in slowly, hold for the length of a breath, breathe out slowly, rest for the length of a breath.
6. On the inhale, say the first part of the mantra "I am myself" with your internal voice. During the held breath, hold this thought as well and let it fill you; let it permeate your being with acceptance and certainty.
7. On the exhale, say the second part of the mantra "alone in All" with your internal voice. During the rest period, relax into this thought.
8. As images, sensations, feelings, or thoughts arise, let them go and return to the mantra.
9. If you become disquieted, uncomfortable, jittery, or severely disoriented, try to relax through it. If uncomfortable sensations persist or become extreme, cease all meditation for the day.
10. Give yourself space after your meditation to process what you have experienced. Just *be* with what has happened without judgment or a sense of conclusion.

Stimulating Intuition – Journaling

Journaling connects us with our thoughts and emotions in a way that can be both fun and intense. To spend a half-hour each day writing about our life – the reactions and reflections of our day-to-day existence, or just the random cogitations and images that appear in our mind – peels the onion of our experience down to its core, so that with each new sentence we come closer to our personal truths. I am always surprised by what springs forth when I write, as if I am having a conversation with someone I thought I knew very well, but find they are sharing things I never would have expected. This kind of revelation can be achieved with any creative self-expression.

Daily Reflections

Perusing the list on pages 49-50, can you find some Just for Today reflections that contradict each other? If you can identify a group of seemingly incongruent ideas, begin to incorporate as many of these concepts as possible into a daily routine. Allow them adequate space in your mind and heart to coexist despite apparent opposition. Notice what happens to these ideas – and your own thought process – when you allow them to peacefully coexist within you.

As you begin integrating all the Just for Today concepts, avoid letting your reflection become an empty habit, a rote exercise. Change the order of recitation. Try breathing in each idea, then breathing them out. Take time to reconsider each phrase, weigh each word, and understand each principle on an emotional, spiritual and practical level. The more you allow these themes to indwell you – and the more you allow yourself to dwell in the present moment of alert consideration – the more this practice will come alive for you.

4 - HARMONIZING ACTION AND INTENTION

No matter how far along we are in our journey, we are always in for a surprise. Our will – that is, the energy of volition, which we generate each and every second – has a concrete effect in the physical realm that can exceed our wildest imagination. Evidence of this could be called "being in the flow," "synchronicity," "being in tune," "staying on the path," or "creating our own reality." These are often a direct result of the quality, clarity, and sincerity of intentions in concert with the discipline of mind, heart, spirit and will. As we observe such *artifacts of will* it is essential that we avoid fixating on them to guide our way or affirm our beliefs, for that would constitute attachment, distract us from our purpose, and interfere with the mechanisms of fulfillment. In a way, the more our intentions are manifested around us, the less we should embrace their significance. Still, the hallmark of a true mystic is the powerful materialization of the good of All in every thought, word and deed – an uncanny harmonization of action and intention.

What is actually happening here? Are there spiritual intelligences at work? Are there quantum agents ready to jump at the pure intensity of our thoughts? Is there some psychic organ awakened within us through mystical practice? As fascinating as these questions are, they should be of less interest to us than our state of mind and heart as we move forward. What matter most are patience, humility, love, gratitude, compassion, mindfulness, and perseverance. And something else: being able to maintain a *neutrality of will.* Like the mental stillness that precedes advanced contemplative states, or the quiet plenitude of heart that sustains the golden intention, or the calm certainty of being one with the All, an ability to keep our will at rest is a necessary step along the mystic's way. This is, to a large degree, what governs the scope of our conscious and unconscious impact in the world.

There are three prerequisites to harmonizing actions and intentions in the most positive way, and they echo the first three core disciplines of mysticism:

- A fearless openness and unhinging of our psyche in connecting with our True Self through mystical perception-cognition

- A relaxation of our own acquisitiveness, and a generosity of spirit that intentionally aligns itself with the good of All

- An ability to remain humble, detached and without expectation, and grateful all at the same time – a disposition solidified by identifying our individual Self with the transpersonal and transcendent

The fourth necessary quality is neutrality of will. This state is as simple and difficult to describe or attain as mystical union. It is not that we fervently desire something, or that we reject one possibility in favor of another. It is that we sense the rightness of a clear consequence through spiritual cognizance and relax into its inevitability. It is like having sincere acceptance and gratitude about the now, and readily acknowledging the perfection of the Universe with wonder in our hearts, then quietly offering our own energy to the eternal celebration. Once again, it is a kind of letting go, a condition born of our new identity where we surrender control while remaining expansively aware. In this way, "action without action" is easily understood, as are achievement through simply being, the spontaneous fulfillment of desire, miraculous prayer, and the nature of synchronicity. These are all facets of the same gem – we must simply become that gem.

We might call this process "wishing without wanting." I wish for something I intuitively know benefits the good of All, even as it nourishes me, *but I do not want it.* That is, I do not yearn for it, I do not feel I need it, and I do not believe that without my effort all Light will cease to shine in this realm of existence. At the same time, I am the Light, and the Light is me, and what I imagine for myself and others is less a fantasy of what could be, and more a natural transmutation of that Light into a dialogue of heart, mind and action. I am that I am, It is that It is, and All That Happens is a normative consequence of those conditions. Is there fate, predetermination, or a life-contract that frames the borders of our volition, just as mortality appears to frame our corporeal existence? Perhaps these are temporary boundaries of Self, but if we maintain the golden intention, persistent compassion, and gratitude for what is...why does it matter? How could we ever be disappointed, thwarted or misdirected if we have let go of ego and impetuous self-gratification? This is how wishing without wanting works.

Lastly, it is also important to differentiate neutrality of will from both annihilation and subjugation of will – neither of which leads to the same place. Many common artifacts of will are described in more detail in the Appendix, but neutrality of will is what we should be most concerned with, especially at the onset of mystical practice. Here we are not suppressing desire, we are letting it go. We are not forcing our mind in one direction or other, we are easing into a receptive quiet. We are not stressfully striving toward some end, we are being diligent and watchful and joyfully alive to ourselves as we tune in to the wisdom of the Universe.

Culmination in a Peculiar Quality of Consciousness

As we fortify the four core disciplines of mysticism, we increasingly give up our willfulness and tend less and less to react from ego, needy emotion or other rudimentary impulses. Spiritual cognizance, a passionate caring, and identification with the All converge into a profound sense of harmony within and without. This sense of harmony, in turn, leads to a peculiar quality of consciousness. Among the chief characteristics of this consciousness are two things: a strong sense of centeredness amid the varied forces tugging at our mind, heart spirit and will; and what I would describe as a continuous spiritual dialogue with the Source of Light and Life. Respectively, I call these the *art of suspension* and *praying without ceasing*. In both cases, the internal shift is one of relationship – in one case between the essence of Self and the essence of the Universe, and the other between our intentional mind and everything we perceive.

As with any relationship, mystical interdependencies flourish within love, openness and reinforced connection. Likewise, most difficulties arise when we are dishonest, stop listening, or place egoistically distorted wants ahead of mutual nourishment. In praying without ceasing, our being is therefore trustingly receptive and infinitely giving. In the art of suspension, our interior landscape rests in permeable stillness, devoid of compulsion or predisposition, and all directions of thought and action are equidistant for us. And it does not matter how we choose to conceive of our own being or the Source to strengthen these relationships. We might believe our essence is composed of spirit, or transmuted life force, or conscious energy, or biochemical reactions, or an expression of the Soul. We might conceive of the Source as Deity, Universal Essence, Vital Continuum or Infinite Mystery. Such conceptions are trapped in the context of our experience, and in all likelihood only dimly reflect the actuality. But when we have tasted the Sacred through gnosis, and when our spiritual intelligence is supported by a transformed identity, then we no longer require specific beliefs to immerse ourselves in miraculous connection. We have discovered the wholly integrated One, and engender separateness only to facilitate the quality of communication, life lessons, and development of character that relationships provide.

In this way, a mystic suspends an increasingly potent intentional mind in a web of widening possibilities, so that through careful discernment we can always contribute to spiritually healthy outcomes. And even in moments of greatest darkness, even when we stumble and forget the nature of our interconnection, we remain joined with the Source in an intimate, transparent conversation.

Thus we are always able to invoke the perpetual orbital dance of heart, mind, spirit and will that abides in stillness; or rather, through stillness we recognize the holy dance that has always been within us, and can joyfully gift our talents to its immanent purpose.

Risks and Benefits

Are there potentially negative outcomes if we are not careful with our will? Assuredly there are, and thankfully we can learn from them. For the artifacts of will we generate can certainly be antagonistic to our well-being. We might make ourselves sick, or manifest something spiritually antagonistic in our life, or inadvertently sabotage ourselves in one or more of our goals. The power of our will is such that fear, self-defeatism, low self-esteem, confusion, delusion, and ego can undermine positive potential. That is why learning how to moderate our will and guide it with mindful, all-embracing love-consciousness is so important. That is why we should remain carefully attentive to every whim of our minds and every wish of our hearts.

Words tend to fall short when describing mystical realities, and as with so many truths, experience is not just the best teacher, it is really the only teacher. Otherwise, it is easy for our wonderfully creative imaginations to delude us into thinking we know something we do not. As Aldous Huxley put it, "knowledge is a function of being." But at the heart of a neutral will is complete freedom – from runaway desires, overconfident assertions, foolish expectations and egotism. In the same way, a mystic who embraces the art of suspension has an invaluable tool for their journey and a window into future stages of being. Similarly, when praying without ceasing arises, embryonic faith no longer smacks of artifice.

Are there measurable results from all of this? Absolutely. Instead of pursuing wisdom, we live wisdom in every moment. Beyond aligning ourselves with the good of All, we become the good of All. More than being illumined, we illuminate everything around us. Instead of loving, we become love. We are in fact setting aside entire toolsets of preparatory spiritual thought and navigation, along with every conclusion we embraced along our path until now, and entering into a freshly vulnerable unknown; an entirely new kind of existence.

This concludes our discussion of the four core disciplines. Before continuing on, I encourage you to revisit the exercises at the end of chapters 1-4 to round out your understanding. The next section covers additional practices designed to expand consciousness, relax and heal the body, energize the spirit, and help us discover through direct experience our true nature and purpose in this life. We will also examine other life consequences of choosing the mystic's way. How might it impact our relationships or responsibilities to community? How will we grow and how can we measure that progress? All of these are closely connected to the shaping of our will and the many ways it evidences itself inside and around us. With persistence, each of us can arrive at our most spiritually profitable state, where we continually contribute to the good of All with both humility and confidence.

Different Perspectives on Action and Intention

"The softest stuff in the world overcomes the firmest. The insubstantial enters where there is no space. By this I know the benefit of something achieved by simply being. Few in the world can understand accomplishment apart from action, and instruction where there are no words."
– Lao Tzu

"In short, remember this: that whatever you prize which is beyond your will, you have inasmuch destroyed your will."
– Epictetus

"For if you carefully eliminate contentious arguments, you will discover the truth that the Mind, the Soul of God, rules over All – over Fate, over Law, over everything – and that nothing is impossible for it."
– *Corpus Hermeticum*

"When your will is connected to God's will, when your thoughts are connected to Divine thoughts, when your words bring you nearer to the Infinite, and when your actions are effortless, you are more apt to succeed."
– Shoni Labowitz

"As long as we have a body, we cannot renounce action altogether. True renunciation is giving up all desire for personal reward."
– *Bhagavad Gita* (Eknath Easwaran)

"If the impact of any spiritual experience is to increase humility and cause one to become more other-concerned and compassionate, it can probably be assumed that the integration of the experience is moving in a creative direction. But if the impact is to increase self-concern and self-importance; if it makes one feel distanced from rather than closer to other people; and if it stifles rather than encourages humble compassion; one should be suspicious."
– Gerald G. May

"The goal now, as audacious as it sounds, is not merely to transcend the world but to transform the world, to become an agent of the evolutionary impulse itself. Indeed, in surrendering one's ego to that, one literally feels oneself being filled up with a divine and luminous energy and a passion to transform the world and the whole Universe for a cause that has nothing to do with oneself."
– Andrew Cohen

"If you live your life in me, and my words live in your hearts, ask whatever you wish and it shall come true for you."
– *Gospel of John*

"Even as you bring your intentions and desires into conscious awareness, surrender the outcome to nature. Cultivate an attitude of trusting that when things are not going exactly the way you intend them to, there is a grander design at work."
– Deepak Chopra & David Simon

Concept Affinity: Artifacts of Will

Zen Buddhism	Christian Mysticism	Kabbalah	Sufism	Taoism	Kundalini Yoga
Abhinna	Pneumatika	Netzach Hod Yesod	Karamat	Gǎn Yìng (Stimulus-Response)	Siddhi

Sample Mystic Activators

Mantra Meditation – Part Two (with Visualization)

1. Objective: Between 15 and 75 minutes of continuous meditation each day. If you can, insulate this with a buffer of five minutes before and after. It is best to practice this meditation only after several weeks practicing Part One.

2. Find a quiet place to sit and relax, and begin your meditation with an inner commitment to the golden intention.

3. Relax every part of your body. Start with your hands and feet – perhaps moving them or shaking them a little to release tension – then your arms and legs, then your torso, head and neck.

4. Breathe deeply and evenly into your stomach, preferably through the nose, so that your shoulders remain still but your stomach "inflates." Practice this until you are comfortable with it.

5. Begin the "four-fold" breath – that is: breathe in slowly, hold for the length of a breath, breathe out slowly, rest for the length of a breath.

6. On the inhale, say the first part of the mantra "The Sacred Soul" with your internal voice. During the held breath, hold this thought and let it fill you.

7. On the exhale, say the second part of the mantra "in All is One" with your internal voice. During the rest period, relax into this thought; let it permeate your being with acceptance and certainty.

8. As images, sensations, feelings, or thoughts arise, let them go and return to the mantra.

9. As you become comfortable residing in this mantra, add a progression of visualizations. First, imagine someone you respect or admire sitting facing you and continue the mantra. After a time, change the visualization to someone with whom you have a loving, mutually respectful relationship. Lastly, change your focus to a person you do not like, who is antagonistic to you or your way of being, or with whom you have not found any common ground. Maintain your visualization of each person for as long as possible.

10. If you become disquieted, uncomfortable, jittery, or severely disoriented, try to relax through it. If uncomfortable sensations persist or become extreme, cease all meditation for the day.

11. Give yourself space after your meditation to process what you have experienced. Just *be* with what has happened without judgment or a sense of conclusion.

Stimulating Intuition – Listening to Now

1. If you live near trees, find a comfortable place to sit among them and listen to the wind whisper through the branches. Close your eyes and let the wind-song fill your mind, letting all other sounds fade away. Now imagine the wind itself coursing through your body. As the breeze moves through you, does it have a texture or pattern? Do its patterns change? If you listen very carefully, is there perhaps a message there in the changing melody, in the breathing of the sky? If you live near a beach, try the same exercise with the surging rhythms of ocean waves. If near a river or stream, try it with the sound of flowing water. It is ideal if there are few people or distractions around you, but even if there is distraction, see if you can listen so intently that Nature speaks to you more loudly than anything else.

2. There are countless ways to pay attention to the subtle sensations of our bodies. One approach is to simply ask ourselves where we physically experience wants or emotions. What parts of your body react to different thoughts and intentions? Where do you feel hunger, anger, sleepiness,

excitement, disappointment, happiness or fatigue? What are the characteristics of these sensations? As we become attuned to our somatic self, we can more readily notice messages expressed as a tightening of muscles, a sharp intake of breath, a rush of heat through the chest, or a tingling at the back of the neck. Listening to the language of our bodies is yet another avenue of intuitive sensitivity.

Daily Reflections

If you have already spent concerted time and effort working with the list on pages 49-50, try committing all of the Just for Todays to memory. See how many you can recall in your daily practice without referencing the list. When you have finished your reflections, look at the list to see which ones you have forgotten. The following day, spend extra time thinking about those forgotten few. Try to examine each phrase from as many different angles as possible. Moving forward, mix up the order and see if you can still remember all of them.

One way of measuring the impact of your reflective practice is to evaluate whether it changes or refines your actions and reactions over time. Before you go to sleep each night, think back on some of the memorable events of your day. Were there any situations that triggered responses from you that might have benefited from applying a particular Just for Today? Can you identify areas where the concepts or values inherent to your reflective practice were clearly expressed? Is the genuine intention of your practice harmonizing with your actions and reactions?

Lastly, if you find yourself gravitating toward a particular group of Just for Todays – or, alternatively, struggling to remember a particular group – ask yourself why that might be. Mysticism is mainly about inquiring into our innermost Self. Thinking about why we react certain ways, or why we have attraction or aversion to certain concepts, will lay the groundwork for ever-deepening insight.

5 – APPLICATIONS AND CONSEQUENCES

Additional Mystic Activator Examples

The following are some intermediate-level mystic activators I have offered in my courses. They generally require a more thorough grounding in the golden intention than earlier exercises, as well as a quality of concentration that is easier once introductory activators have been mastered. Each of them falls under one or more of the four categories already described:

- Subtractive Meditation
- Ecstatic Induction
- Symbolic and Synchronistic Ritual
- Perfection of Love

Although anyone can try such exercises, each is still likely to appeal more to one type of person than another, and most will yield significant results only after daily practice over a period of weeks or months. Sometimes an approach will become more useful once we progress into a new phase of personal development, so if something does not work for you at first, try it again later. From the perspective of a balanced integral practice, it will also be important over time to either regularly revisit all four types of activators, or to integrate them all into a single routine. But regardless of how we access the mystical, it is critical to remember that any change in consciousness is like inviting a magical creature to sit beside us for a while – nothing can be forced into being or made to conform to our expectations. If we truly let go, we will be surprised and humbled, and much of what our ego cherishes will be left behind. Always, the mystical experience is more about relinquishment than personal gain.

Most of the mystic activators in this book could be loosely categorized as meditation, but there is nevertheless quite a variety, each with its own emphasis. For instance, some practices enhance our ability to concentrate on a single focus or promote a particular emotional state, while others are a general reflection on themes or concepts. Some are mainly a means of inquiring into Self, while others cultivate a sense of mindfulness – a non-reactive attentiveness to what is occurring within and without. More than anything, introducing meditative discipline into our daily lives nurtures us on many levels. Our self-awareness and emotional intelligence improve. Our self-esteem is enhanced. Our understanding of compassion is deepened, and our ability to express it from moment to moment is powerfully facilitated. We become peaceful, centered, and alert, with healing benefits to our minds, hearts and bodies. Eventually, an ever more complete spiritual cognizance will well up to fill a gently receptive interior spaciousness.

Self-Care Meditation

1. Objective: Between 15 and 75 minutes of continuous meditation each day. If you can, insulate this with a buffer of five minutes before and after.
2. Find a quiet place to sit and relax, and begin your meditation with an inner commitment to the golden intention.

3. Relax every part of your body. Start with your hands and feet – perhaps moving them or shaking them a little to release tension – then your arms and legs, then your torso, head and neck.

4. Breathe deeply and evenly into your stomach, preferably through the nose, so that your shoulders remain still but your stomach "inflates." Practice this until you are comfortable.

5. Lay one hand over the other (with the physically dominant hand – the right hand for most – on top) on the surface of your breastbone in the middle of your chest, so that the palm of your sub-dominant hand is placed over your heart chakra.

6. Begin the four-fold breath, maintaining attention on the heart chakra as the locus of your emotional self.

7. Begin to project a gentle, loving energy into your heart chakra. Really care for this self-reference as unconditionally, openly and fearlessly as you can.

8. Maintain this state for as long as possible, letting go of any other images, thoughts, sounds or sensations that enter your attention, always returning to the caring for Self meditation.

9. If you become disquieted, uncomfortable, jittery, or severely disoriented, try to relax through it. If uncomfortable sensations persist or become extreme, cease all meditation for the day.

10. Give yourself space after your meditation to process what you have experienced. Just *be* with what has happened without judgment or a sense of conclusion.

First Invocation

1. Objective: Between 15 and 75 minutes of continuous meditation each day. If you can, insulate this with a buffer of five minutes before and after.
2. Find a quiet place to sit and relax, and begin your meditation with an inner commitment to the golden intention.
3. Relax every part of your body. Start with your hands and feet – perhaps moving them or shaking them a little to release tension – then your arms and legs, then your torso, head and neck.
4. Breathe deeply and evenly into your stomach, preferably through the nose, so that your shoulders remain still but your stomach "inflates." Practice this until you are comfortable with it.
5. Lightly hook your hands together in front of you, fingertips-to-palm in a yin/yang clasp.[5] Place your sub-dominant hand (the left hand for most) over the dominant hand.
6. Relax your body and breathe deeply into your stomach (ideally in through the nose and out through the mouth)
7. Mentally focus on the middle Tan Tien (the heart center in the middle of the upper torso – not to be confused with the heart chakra) as a point or tiny sphere of bright yellowy-white light.
8. Begin the four-fold breath, maintaining focus on the middle Tan Tien, and direct the words of your mantra there. On the inhale, repeat inwardly: "Let Love and Light arise in All that Is...." (receptive element) And on the exhale: "and All That Is arise in Love and Light ...." (active element)
9. If your concentration wanders from the mantra or from your middle Tan Tien, gently return your attention to both of them.

---

[5] This is not a traditional yin/yang mudra, but is intended to help integrate receptive and active elements of the meditation.

10. After several separate sessions where a steady centering in the middle Tan Tien and mantra is achieved, begin to broaden your focus while maintaining the mantra. Always begin with your heart center, and then expand your awareness out into your immediate environment, toward people you know (and specifically their Tan Tiens), toward places where suffering is occurring, toward your political leaders, toward the Earth as a whole, toward the subatomic fabric of space-time, and so on....

11. If you become disquieted, uncomfortable, jittery, or severely disoriented, try to relax through it. If uncomfortable sensations persist or become extreme, cease all meditation for the day.

12. Give yourself space after your meditation to process what you have experienced. Just *be* with what has happened without judgment or a sense of conclusion.

Contemplating Presence and Absence

1. Objective: Between 15 and 75 minutes of deep contemplation each day. If you can, insulate this with a buffer of five minutes before and after.

2. Find a quiet place to sit comfortably. Start your contemplation with an inner commitment to the golden intention.

3. Relax your body and breathe deeply into your stomach (in through the nose, out through the mouth)

4. Imagine yourself as a compassionate and caring spirit that is observing things in your day-to-day life from outside your body. You have no way to directly impact events, you just observe them. Think about yesterday, and consider how your physical form – the person others perceive as "you" – interacted with people, places and things throughout the day. Try to be a non-judgmental witness of everything that occurred.

5. Still in a spirit form outside of your body, imagine how your day will be tomorrow. Observe your physical form interacting with people, places and things. Without judgment, follow the course of the day to its end.

6. Now go back to yesterday. This time, as a compassionate and caring spirit without a body or the ability to influence events, imagine how the day would have progressed if your physical

form had been absent. Imagine your workplace, your close friends and family, your intimate relationships, the place where you live – all passing through time as if your physical presence was no longer there.

7. Repeat this exercise with tomorrow in mind. Imagine how all the people, places and things in your life would be if they passed through time without your being there, and perhaps never having known or encountered you.

8. Finally, return to the present. As a compassionate and caring spirit, still outside of your body, observe your physical form here in this space for a few moments. Then, imagine this space with your physical form absent. You are still here in spirit, but you cannot be perceived and you cannot effect change. Remain in this state of spiritual observation for as long as you can.

9. If you become distracted at any point, go back to the beginning of the last phase of the exercise and start over.

10. If you become disquieted, uncomfortable, jittery, or severely disoriented, try to relax through it. If uncomfortable sensations persist or become extreme, cease all meditation for the day.

11. Give yourself space after your meditation to process what you have experienced. Just *be* with what has happened without judgment or a sense of conclusion.

Returning to Emptiness

One of the most powerful – and difficult – mystic activators is a kind of non-meditation. Just sit comfortably, close your eyes, and let yourself be still. For many of us, our thoughts, emotions and physical sensations will command our interest. But if we free that attention entirely from any specific focus, and settle into a receptive quiet from which all stimuli – the chatter of our thoughts, the aching in our muscles, the sounds around us, the emotional tension of our day – fall away from conscious consideration, we begin to intuit what really exists within the remaining silence. As with all previous exercises, it is important to avoid forcing our minds into or away from anything. Instead, begin by being attentive to each feeling, thought or sensation that arises, resting in them a while without reacting to them. Just let them be. Then, as naturally and effortlessly as they have arisen, let them go. A bird rises on invisible currents, its wings unmoving, then vanishes from sight. When cradled in the golden intention, such letting go is a returning to emptiness, an utterly open and unrestricted means to spiritual cognizance.

"Just for Today" Daily Reflections

These reflections can be a standalone practice or used to augment other mystical exercises. You might enjoy reciting them each morning while going for a walk – a continuous walking reflection of perhaps thirty minutes. After speaking each phrase aloud or silently, listen to the silence afterwards, noticing the reactions of your heart, mind, body and spirit. When finished, open yourself to whatever is around you and revel in the present. In the evening, try repeating this process as a reconsideration of your day. Each reflection can be directed toward ourselves, toward others, toward all that we understand to exist, toward a deity we worship, or even toward the unknown. There are therefore many implications for each phrase. Repeating the reflections, each time with a unique audience or objective in mind (or none at all) can evoke new meaning and have surprising impact on our lives even after years of repetition.

1. Just for today, patience and acceptance in all things
2. Just for today, nothing has to be wrong
3. Just for today, acknowledgment without prejudice in every situation
4. Just for today, courage to be compassionate and kind to all
5. Just for today, embracing the Natural Realm as part of Self, with honor and respect for all
6. Just for today, remembering the well-being of others, nourishing them through being well
7. Just for today, transforming all things into the good of All
8. Just for today, faith which far exceeds all hopes, desires and fears

9. Just for today, insight and understanding into fruitful conduct
10. Just for today, listening from stillness, and seeing what is
11. Just for today, confidence without arrogance, and humility without passivity
12. Just for today, clarity and sincerity in purpose and intentions
13. Just for today, balance in caring for the house of Self and all the selves within
14. Just for today, tranquility in relinquishing ego, and flowing with the Source of Life and Light
15. Just for today, a generous spirit, free from attachment and expectation
16. Just for today, being in the now, without illusions
17. Just for today, honesty and integrity in all situations
18. Just for today, thoughts and words that edify, encourage and inspire
19. Just for today, with each breath, breathing in wholeness and vitality
20. Just for today, diligence and mindfulness in every moment
21. Just for today, persisting gratitude from the heart, and celebration in every action and interaction
22. Just for today, filled with Divine laughter, the heart sings
23. Just for today, ease and simplicity in every choice
24. Just for today, a living example with conviction and contentment
25. Just for today, creating something, destroying nothing
26. Just for today, great care with whims and wishes
27. Just for today, the soul is never compromised

Measuring Our Progress

Getting wrapped up in measuring, comparing, or tracking our mystical progress is fairly counterproductive to a spiritually profitable existence, and there is sometimes too little difference between healthy self-awareness and obsessive self-centeredness. I have found the following adages to be helpful in remembering this fact, and frequently revisit them:

1. We are seldom if ever as far along as we think we are.
2. It is a rare and precious thing for us to grasp the true meaning of any experience in our lives.
3. The more eager our expectation of outcomes from interior mystical discipline, the more predictable our falling short of them will be.

In any journey, to enhance our self-awareness and keep ourselves on track, it is nevertheless useful to have an idea of where we are going and what some of the milestones along the way might look like. One method of examining our progress is a contemplative-emotive model of learning, in which we observe the impact of mystical practice on our state of consciousness and our ability to translate convictions into action. A common progression of contemplative states and the cycle of emotional transformation are outlined in the chart on the next page.

Keep in mind that merely exercising mystical muscles without a clear direction in mind can become, as Thomas Merton once described it, nothing more than "consecrated narcissism." It is therefore imperative that we understand and embrace our reasons for pursuing personal transformation, and continually reevaluate our chosen course. One application for the contemplative-emotive method is to consider what the "good of All" really means. Do you think it is important? Can you hold it at your center, allowing all thoughts, emotions and actions to flow out from it? Beginning there, observe what happens as you work through each of the contemplative-emotive steps. Does your understanding of the good of All evolve? Does the context and meaning of your efforts shift?

The Contemplative-Emotive Learning Process

Contemplative States	Cycle of Emotional Transformation
1. **Simple Reflection:** We become consciously aware of all phenomena and begin reflecting on them.	1. **Recognition:** We recognize and acknowledge our current emotional state.
2. **Contemplative Self-Awareness:** We become consciously aware of the process of *simple reflection* as it occurs in us from moment-to-moment, observing and evaluating the qualities of this process.	2. **Examination:** Without judgment or overreaction, we examine and accept our emotions.
	3. **Admission:** We admit to ourselves that change would be beneficial – that having a different emotional state would be more healthy and productive.
3. **Suspended Valuation:** We intentionally suspend valuation altogether, and just observe our experiences, thoughts, feelings and physical sensations without placing them in the context of our values, beliefs or assumptions.	
	4. **Detachment:** We let go of the counterproductive feelings – that is, relax our emotional state until is greatly diminished, or dissipates completely. We may also choose to relinquish some of the underlying beliefs or assumptions that brought this state about.
4. **Non-Thought Awareness:** We let go of both valuations and any thought process, entering into a state of mental, emotional and sensory quiet – even though we may still be consciously observing this state in ourselves, we do not reflect on it.	
5. **Non-Thought Non-Awareness:** We stop acknowledging even the supersensory, just as we did the sensory, and directly experience the bedrock of our own existence – the foundations of our sense of Self and our relationship to the Universe.	5. **Equilibrium:** We achieve a state of neutral and objective calm where we can decide in which emotional direction we wish to go next.
	6. **Commitment:** We choose a specific new emotional direction and begin to actuate that state.
6. **Non-Being Awareness:** We cease to discriminate between the state of non-thought non-awareness and any independently constructed sense of Self – we come to identify ourselves with this state and thus develop a subjective submersion in "non-being."	7. **Action:** We facilitate and support the newly chosen state with reinforcing actions, thoughts, beliefs, experiences, etc.
7. **Non-Being Non-Awareness:** Where self-awareness and other-awareness – and any acknowledgement of subject and object – completely evaporate.	

Every spiritual tradition has different descriptions and numbers of developmental states, stations or stages, and usually details other subsets of characteristics – emphasizing heart over mind, mind over heart, transcendent sense over heart and mind, etc. However, the contemplative-emotive model occurs in nearly all of them. Without being distracted by self-consciousness, we can use it to track our exploration of the unknown. Try implementing emotional transformation as part of mystical practice by journaling your epiphanies, intuitions and self-discoveries, then committing to act from each new altitude of understanding. Evaluate the results after following through and decide if you want to support each new direction. In the contemplative vein, advancing meditation will introduce you to all seven contemplative states, so journaling your progress there may also be helpful. At first, movement through emotional and contemplative threads will seem like separate experiences, and perhaps come in fits and starts. Over time, all of this will merge into one concurrent, interwoven cord that draws you ever onward. As new consciousness becomes comprehension, comprehension becomes doing, doing becomes being, and being becomes consciousness.

The next table contrasts some *spiritually healthy* and *spiritually unhealthy* emotional states – that is, conditions of heart that either contribute to, or interfere with, our spiritual evolution. These are especially useful in initiating cycles of emotional transformation. Consider some recent events in your life. Have your reactions been spiritually healthy ones? Are there some particular areas you would like to improve? In mysticism we discover a calm center from which we can deliberately choose how to interact with others, and through which we nourish ourselves so that we won't become distracted or depleted. Regardless of the path we choose – intuition exercises, mystic activators, Just for Today reflections, or some combination that works for us – such disciplines will help reinforce all that is spiritually healthy within us. With persistence, we are able to perfect acceptance, kindness and compassion first for ourselves and then for everyone and everything around us. Quiescent in this unconditional love-consciousness, we are then able to make wise and discerning choices much more consistently.

Spiritual Health of Emotional States

Spiritually Healthy State	Spiritually Unhealthy State
Courage to defend the well-being of Self and others, with patience and forbearance	Indignant, self-righteous rage, which is easily provoked and unconcerned about the damage it inflicts
Compassionate desire to nourish others with wisdom and kindness, while at the same time sustaining our own well-being	Compulsive need to rescue others without considering our own well-being or what is truly best for those being "rescued"
Love that has no conditions or expectations attached to it, and that patiently accepts another's shortcomings	A desire to control disguised as attention and devotion, but which impatiently demands specific reciprocation
Self-controlled ordering of effort according to what is most important (via spiritual discernment and intuitive insight)	Impulsive submission to every urgent or self-indulgent whim without a thought for what is important
Patience for, and an attempt to understand, those who oppose or antagonize us	Fear, paranoia and hatred of things we do not understand
Gratitude and forgiveness	Resentment and divisiveness
Acceptance and flexibility with whatever comes our way	Resistance to change and panic when things seem out of control
Honesty and openness	Avoidance, denial and deception
Peaceful and supportive internal dialogues	Chaotic and demeaning internal dialogues
Admiration and encouragement	Jealousy and criticism
Contentment in any situation, rich or poor, because our focus is on human relationships and developing a wealth of spiritual understanding	Greed and avarice: a compelling desire to possess material power and wealth
Guilt and shame, which resolves into humility and a renewed commitment to growth and maturity	Perpetual, unresolved guilt and shame, which injures self-esteem and cripples any ability to change
Vulnerable and joyful sharing of sexual intimacy in the context of responsible relationships	Wanton lust: an immersion in carnality without considering emotional or spiritual consequences
Mutual inspiration to greater achievement through fair-spirited competition – or better yet, cooperation	Egotistical competitiveness, which craves victory at any cost
Confidence with humility	Self-aggrandizing arrogance
Taking pleasure in the success of others	Taking pleasure in the suffering of others
Hope and faith in positive outcomes	Despair and pessimism: presuming doom

One the one hand, intuitive promptings and mystical epiphanies have little value if they are not integrated into our self-awareness and the purpose and choices of our daily lives. On the other, if we are forever trying to interpret, define and compartmentalize our moments of enlightenment, we may prevent the enrichment of our being by holding on to them too tightly. Ideally, we will continually commit ourselves to actualizing what we encounter in the mystic, while at the same time refreshing our habit of letting go. In this way we can enjoy the delightful and surprising consequences of our new freedoms without becoming attached to them.

Stages of Being

Spiritual evolution is difficult to quantify and is as diverse as humanity itself; however, there are some watershed events that practitioners of many different traditions have observed. One byproduct of the perpetual physiological/experiential/spiritual tug-of-war within us[6] is that we may find ourselves cycling through these evolutions over and over again. Our only real achievement may be in how conscious we are of the stages we are passing through at any given moment, or in the varying amount of effort required to rectify a regressive drift. Sometimes, we plateau at one stage for months – or even years – before continuing on. In my own belief system, our spiritual progress may take many lifetimes. But no matter where I presume myself to be, reflecting on these descriptions often helps identify my next horizon.

1. **Childhood** – The starting point of ignorance. Here we are concerned mostly with primitive urges and self-gratification, with barely a hint of spiritual perception. This is a fairly self-protective phase, while at the same time impulsively adventurous. We are dependent on externals and recklessly reactive, seeking pleasure and ego reinforcement above all else.

2. **First Questions** – We now start sincerely questioning what is, and engage our first insightful surprises about our environment and ourselves. We experience awe and inspiration, and new

---

[6] See *Pyramid of Self* in the Appendix

questions keep arising in us. We suspect there is more to life than stimulation and pleasure, and more to ourselves than animal impulses. This can be unsettling and bewildering, and we may reach out for someone or something to guide us – a mentor, a cultural tradition, or a structured system of belief.

3. **First Awakening** – We are now exposed to our first knowledge beyond the materially obvious – perhaps as a spiritual epiphany or as an unexpected sense of healing or wholeness – and we often react to this with willful resistance. After first tasting awe, we may disregard the raw and powerful insights and emotions triggered by the implications of Spirit. Fear and other primitive impulses quickly assert themselves. As a result, we may rebel against our current beliefs, guides or mentors and seek distraction and solace in more primitive behaviors.

4. **Commitment to Exploration** – Given some time to rebel and relax, we overcome initial resistance and eventually revisit our enhanced awareness and sense of discovery. We decide to follow through on those nagging impulses to explore Spirit. Instead of fear, we now experience euphoric excitement, even while encountering the same insights, ideas and emotions that once frightened us. A feeling of belonging to something greater permeates us, and we investigate with eagerness.

5. **Challenge to Character** – Now we encounter seemingly insurmountable obstacles, causing us to stumble and flounder. We suddenly realize this journey may be more difficult than we expected. Disappointment causes hesitation, and, beleaguered by uncertainties, we might even give up for a time. Spiritual observations and internal shifts of perspective may become too disorienting or seem completely absurd. We may grow numb, or tired, and once again lose our tolerance of risk and our thirst for insight. We may abandon many of our initial hopes about the world and ourselves. We may resist accepting responsibility for our own spiritual well-being and seek comfort or escape.

6. **Recommitment** – Out of our doubts and wariness we return like prodigal offspring to our journey. We accept the limitations

we have uncovered, even as we begin to move beyond them. We take responsibility for the health of our soul and cultivate our first sincere emotional, mental and spiritual disciplines, refining all our senses even as we wean ourselves of dependence on them. We may grieve over our shedding of innocence and the new weight of accountability we feel. There may be emotional pain or existential anxiety over uncomfortable changes, but still we move forward. And as we learn compassion for ourselves, we also develop stronger empathy for others. This, rather than spiritual thirst, is what drives us now.

7. **Potential Derailment** – A subtle but persistent inflation of ego arises within our newfound spiritual confidence. If left unexamined, this can become arrogance. Our journey may now be derailed by pride and overconfidence, and although we feel increasingly informed and empowered, we are really returning to our earliest stage of self-protective ignorance and attachment to the pleasure of our achievements. Our beliefs become a facade for self-indulgence, and we can substantially lose our way in any number of distractions and delusions.

8. **First Freedoms** – At some point an unexpected event reminds us of humility, allowing us to see, perhaps for the first time, how little we really know, how self-absorbed we are, and how short a way we have actually come. A sense of humor is useful here, so we can chuckle at all the serious certainties we have held so dearly. We begin to *completely* let go, offering the outcome of anything we do to the good of All. Ego doesn't compete for our attention as it once did. We set ourselves free from attitudes of needy attachment and discover authentic compassion and objective affection for Self, others, and the realms of Nature and Spirit. In humility, we now become more transparent and open to new ways of being, and several forms of spiritual cognizance may erupt simultaneously within us.

9. **Spiritual Self-Sufficiency** – Although we still have our own identity and ego, these lose importance to us as we become less captivated by our ideas of "self." At the same time, we cease searching outside ourselves for truth, wisdom or strength, and our emotional and spiritual self-reliance grows. We can now

dwell fully in the present, becoming absolutely comfortable with the current moment. A patient, empathetic and kind disposition springs forth from us with ease, and a renewed clarity of purpose permeates our day-to-day life. We continue the very difficult work of healing ourselves on the most fundamental levels, often with an unnerving honesty and insight. And we share that healing with others through how we unselfconsciously are – as opposed to what we consciously do. Any lingering urge to be judgmental or even differentiate between people vanishes. We embrace profound respect and admiration for all things, and spontaneously manifest an encouraging and edifying presence for everything and everyone in our lives.

10. **Union and Alienation** – Barriers to our communion with All that Is break down completely. Enduring connection with every aspect of the Sacred – our True Self, the realms of Nature, other people, spiritual intelligences, and even the unimagined and unknowable – becomes simple and transparent to us. Because of this connection, we understand more clearly the characteristics of our shared human condition, the purpose of Spirit, and the patterns of creation all around us. Our wisdom deepens. Our own spiritual directedness is sharpened. This can be isolating, because many of the mundane habits in which we heartily engaged (and which others we care about may still think important) lose their allure. Also, our wisdom and assertions, though clear and obvious to us, might seem like nonsense to others. Because of this, we may feel alienated, sad, or even agitated and angry – despite the wonders and miracles we constantly seem to be witnessing. And so we should pay special attention to nourishing and nurturing ourselves on every level, remaining committed to our spiritual practice and sharing our journey with other spiritually minded people.

11. **The Great Choice** – At this stage we are faced with a decision: to remain engaged with the world – that is, society with its acquisitive and sensual orientation – or to exit the world. In part, this is influenced by our commitments to partnership, family and community. It is nevertheless tempting to sharply

reduce interaction with the physical realm, perhaps because we have become so intensely aware of conditions and forces at work within it, and because there are other ways of being now available to us. For example, we might wish to pursue continuous meditation and reflection, exploring new insights and awakenings without a care for what goes on around us. We might want to hermit ourselves away in the wilderness. We might be tempted to leave the material plane altogether. We realize we have complete freedom at this point (we have always had this potential, but now we fully understand it), but like any other type of personal empowerment, we hope to use our freedom wisely. At this milestone in our evolution we must reshape and renew the primary focus of our lives, even as we question the importance of who we are and what we do.

12. **Compassionate Service** – However we remain in the world, we decide to help transform it, aligning ourselves with all that is healing, loving and creative. How can we encourage the spiritual life of others? How can we bring compassion and healing to the suffering? How can we contribute to works of good for All? We now act from a place of innately apprehending the answers to these questions. At this stage we are still susceptible to drifting from our course and might even revisit old patterns of thought and behavior. Why? Because even though we are more fully actuating our purpose, our commitment to the Sacred still benefits from daily renewal. Also, there can be pain over the continued stripping away of our previous conceptions of *what is*. We may even grieve over losing the spiritual excitement – or intimacy with previous conceptions of the Divine – we once experienced. What helps us most at this time is that although we no longer clutch at accomplishment for our sense of security, we continually actuate our newfound purpose. Paradoxically, this is both a time of challenging and far-reaching decisions, and an easy and commanding ability to act. And, of course, there are always a few deep-seated fears and vulnerabilities we continue to address, though fewer than when we began. I think this stage of being is almost like another childhood, where we stand on the threshold of a whole new type of journey, and a whole new approach to our existence. At the same time, it is the beginning

of true spiritual adulthood, where we have at long last learned the value of transcendent selflessness.

13. **Harmonized Existence** – Like cresting a tremendous wave in our passage, we now enter into ever-deepening continuum of unconditional love-consciousness, and with it a comprehensive sense of peace and simplicity. We become like a piece of bread soaked with spiritual honey, perpetually replenished. All our goals and desires are consumed in the effortlessness of passionately and compassionately being. We have both nothing more to accomplish and an endless number of tasks before us, and there is only quiet contentment, unquestioning strength, and sincere humility in the face of the Absolute. Every action becomes a sharing of our essence, which in turn has come to identify itself with the essence of All Things. We more easily maintain a hyperextended, all-inclusive consciousness that prevents disruption or misdirection, and mundane doubts evaporate. Because of a now persistent contentment, infusive joy and overall spiritual health, we often don't think to look further. However, as with many previous stages of being, the next horizon may come upon us suddenly and unbidden, and all that we require to meet it is patience, resolve and courage.

14. **Consummate Acquiescence** – We tend to squirm away from the first glimpses of this stage, just as we may have avoided others early on, because it challenges and dissolves the last vestiges of our identity – both personal and Universal. Even subjective identification with the Absolute is displaced by something more distilled: an ever-present All-Being that pierces the very quiddity of existence. Here we encounter the bedrock of reality where we completely inhabit our own soul; that is, we submerge ourselves in the entirety of the Divine Spark itself, with all its infinite possibilities. We no longer know, or feel, or sense – we *become*. Where previously our lives were infused with unconditional compassion, now the will to love is eradicated within a raw, unadorned presence of the Most Sacred: there is no will, there are only the foundations of things – of love, and will, and even the Life Force itself – in which we flow and which flow through us. Like a cup of water emptied

into a lake, we have utterly forgotten Self, becoming both the lake and the empty cup. All barriers are gone – all predispositions, all fears, all aspirations, all measurements; even thought itself is subjugated to completely being. There cannot be differentiation any longer: the farthest reaches of the Universe are equal to the nearest object; a sense of vastness is equivalent to a sense of closeness; the beginnings and ends of space-time have no reference other than elemental continuity; the order and relationship of All that Is melts into an entirety which transcends the cosmos itself. Even nothingness and somethingness – even life and death – share common ground in our awareness. It is no small understatement to say that this letting go is impossible to put into words, nor can the far-reaching spiritual benefit of living from such a state easily be described. But this stage is available to everyone, is a natural occurrence, and, like all that has gone before, it has always been within us.

Is there more? I am certain there is much more. There are undoubtedly aspects of our journey that reach even beyond the Absolute. Perhaps the Universe itself is but a bubble floating on an endless sea, and the Infinite is but one pebble among millions in a transdimensional landscape beyond imagining. We must continually question and remain open. And as our hearts expand in all directions at once to encompass what we can never completely understand, the most incredible and the most ordinary will keep calling to us from the core of our being, echoing an eternal "*Yes!*"

The Nuances of Synchronicity

Synchronicity in day-to-day life can indicate many things. Early on in our mystical practice, we might notice a confluence of fortuitous events that enhances our spiritual course. It feels like a universal matching funds program: opportunities and resources we could never have anticipated appear with ease; doors open and walls disappear. Often, we create this flow with the quality of our intentions and the neutrality of our will. Later in our journey, synchronicity may indicate other things: that certain choices resonate strongly with our True Self, for instance; or that we are propagating harmony for the benefit of others. But as we mature, external synchronism tends to markedly diminish, replaced by internal and subtle congruities that are far more important to our own growth and the well-being of the Whole. Eventually, the miraculous appears to become an exclusively inward spiral, demanding utmost patience, attentiveness and humility.

There is danger in appreciating synchronicity as accomplishment. If we obsess over synchronistic events, fortifying our self-esteem with them, a counterproductive state I call *dissonant spiritual feedback* is induced. The more we build confidence and security around synchronicity, the louder and more unbearable the squealing distortions of our desires and mystical insights can become. As a result, we may lose ourselves in needy self-obsession and stunt our spiritual growth. Appreciating helpful coincidence is not about justifying that we are good people, that our will is powerful, or that we are on the right evolutionary track; it is about celebration and gratitude when serendipity arrives, then immediately letting go and flowing onward. In the end, the greatest confirmation of spiritual progress is not the accidental or inexplicable, but a generous temperament of heart, a clarity of mind, and a spirit that is as centered and tranquil as it is passionate.

Self-Awareness, Self-Esteem and Self-Nourishment

Mysticism helps us understand who we really are, disrupting our egoistic illusions in favor of the most genuine Self. Every belief about ourselves is challenged, and personas we have constructed to cope with an unreceptive world are cast aside. What remains is a self-perception forged from discernment, honesty and openness. As we come to know ourselves more intimately, we comprehend the glorious Light of our own being and the beauty and awe of Life itself. Our sense of wellness, contentment and harmony with All Things firmly establishes a confident self-esteem. We no longer rely on self-indulgent antics, controlling our surroundings, the affections of others, achieving some material goal, or any other fulfillment of external expectations to feel complete or worthy. We become entirely self-reliant, and anxiety, fear and want are supplanted with thankfulness and compassion. Because of our contact with the foundations of things, with the underlying realities of our own existence and purpose in this life, we have an ever-expanding comprehension of the Self-in-All. This sets us free, and in that freedom we arrive at both serenity and a vigilant and perpetual love-in-action, which in turn nourishes us and everything around us in countless ways.

The Cycle of Personal Growth

Increased awareness of our strengths, limitations, and the many facets of Self	→	Improved compassion for ourselves and others and actions that nourish and support self-esteem
↑		↓
Internal rewards of progressing into higher stages of being and the spiritual and perceptual expansion inherent to that progress	←	Motivation to work for the good of All out of growing respect, gratitude, and emotional strength

To whatever extent we commit ourselves to mystical practice, we are rewarded with a charitable kindness for the True Self we come to know. There are certainly many other avenues we could take to increase self-knowledge, but few provide the clarity of understanding – or the consistent balance of humility and confidence – inherent to the mystic's way. As a component of integral practice or as a standalone investment in personal evolution, mysticism continually adds dimension to our being. This spurs us ever onward, and the natural byproduct of that growth is the enriching transformation of our relationships, our immediate environment and the Universe itself.

What Happens To Our Relationships?

As a mystic, we love our friends without attachment – without clinging to them or our own ideas of what relationship is. Honesty never makes us feel vulnerable, and careful listening is never fraught with impatience, because we have let go of superficiality. When we celebrate the present moment of companionship – as opposed to an anticipated outcome of that moment, or some distant expectation of what our friendship might provide – it is our willingness to invest *right now* that reaps the most precious rewards. Because we are emotionally and spiritually self-reliant, we resist becoming dependent or codependent, and we are clear about what healthy, mutual compassion and nourishment look and feel like. We don't fall into emotionally rescuing others, but are open to sharing tools that will help people help themselves, for we know that every person's well-being is ultimately their own responsibility. And we don't inadvertently overtax, abuse or misuse our friends, because we have joyful consideration for them as part of the All we fervently esteem as Self.

Most importantly, we recognize and accept that we won't receive the sustenance we most deeply crave from other people. This would be like relying on any other external thing for our happiness. On the other hand, the strength we derive from each other can be an enormous benefit during this wonderful shared journey, and having a supportive community within which to trade ideas and experiences generates surprising synergies for the good of All. So, while it is never spiritually healthy to yearn intensely for either isolation or community, it is always beneficial to have a balance of solitude and inspiring friendships and social environments. The mystic's exposure to community will change with time: we may withdraw for a while to focus ourselves, and at other times celebrate life with others and give of ourselves in service. But the connection we have with a group or community is not what sustains us, nor is it our obligation to sustain others; it is instead our celebratory offering to the Universe to both give and receive.

Thus we maintain personal boundaries that are receptive and porous, but nevertheless clearly delineated and firm. I am not suggesting that students of mysticism enforce a safe emotional distance from others or avoid investing themselves in excitingly personal relationships, but rather that as mystics we commit fully and trust completely, without vanquishing our own innate gifts of nourishing ourselves and directing our own spiritual course. In this way the mystic increasingly manifests a genuine Self in the world, leaving behind past modes of dependence or codependence in favor of true interdependence.

Challenging Our Assumptions

One of the distinctive traits of the mystic's way is an almost continuous reassessment of just about everything in light of new mystical information. Whatever we have concluded in the past will be reshaped by successive realizations, and whatever we have held onto for a sense of self-importance crumbles as mystical awareness invites us in new directions. At the least, this can be unnerving and disorienting; at the worst, depressing or even paralyzing. This is why we must keep moving. Mystical practice is not a destination, but a process of constant renewal. To whatever degree we sustain and integrate nondual consciousness – a gnosis of the Absolute – into our daily life, the constructs and illusions we previously relied upon to navigate this world will dissolve into the present moment's truths.

Most of us reflexively assess value and construct meaning in an unconscious way. We resist the neutrality of events – that they are simply what they are until we create meaning around them. Mystical practice promotes a state of mind and heart that is detached from automatic interpretations of reality, is secure in itself, and is able to let go of apparent absolutes in favor of more subtle and provisional associations. We may come to precisely the same conclusions as those suggested by cultural conditioning, spiritual teachings, or the writings of great philosophers. But we will comprehend them much more fully, appreciating the implications and rationale firsthand, as opposed to conforming unquestioningly to habit, tradition, or someone else's ideas.

The following two charts illustrate the transition between an habitual mode of evaluation while navigating new situations, and a more conscious mode of evaluation encouraged by mystical awareness. Through actively assigning meaning, we greet each experience with unconditional acceptance, and a new confidence emerges: that we can deliberately decide the value of something instead of accepting what our automatic thinking tells us. Such a state of neutral awareness – leading first to unconditional acceptance, then to an intentionally interdependent construction of meaning – empowers us to exit the prison of our own confusion and arrogance and open ourselves to *what is, right now*.

Passive Assignment of Meaning

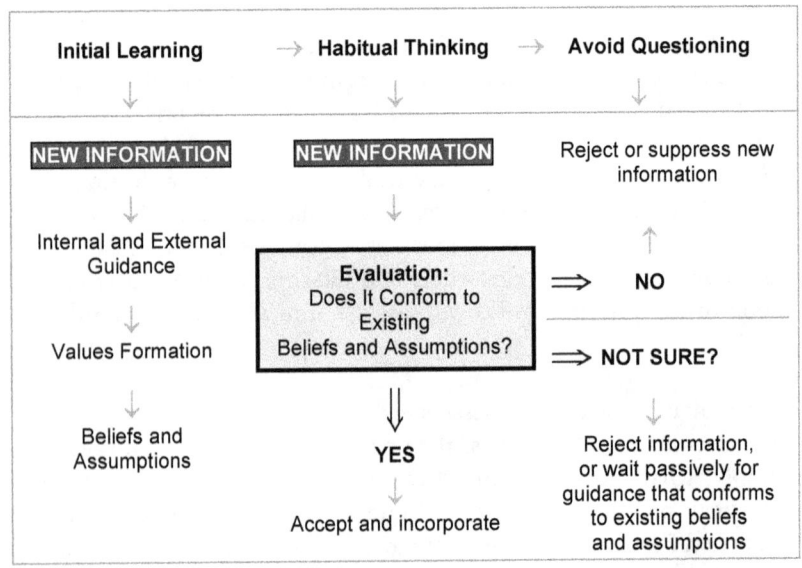

Active Assignment of Meaning

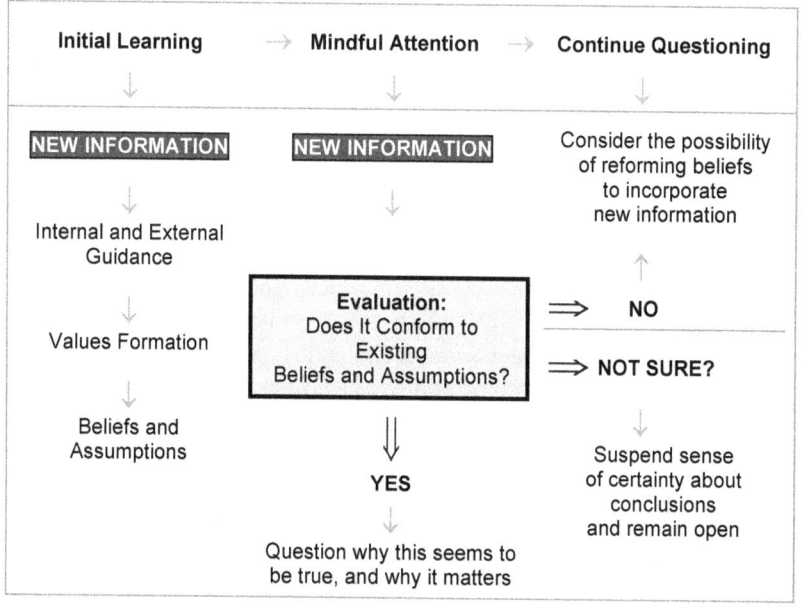

The Nature of Evil

Here are some broad categories of what could be defined as "evil." Each category describes a behavior pattern, but more important are the intentions behind that pattern. Such patterns and intentions do not enhance or support spiritual evolution (already proposed as the definitive "good of All"), but rather seek to undermine and oppose it. We can observe these evidences in ourselves or others, but observation and identification should not equate a judgmental attitude. These descriptions are not intended to condemn any individual or group; on the contrary, all souls struggle in their own way to understand themselves, and each of us shares the same potential for stumbling in the dark. In addition, some of these habits may indicate underlying physiological issues or mental illness. However, I believe whoever knowingly practices such

Essential Mysticism

destructive behaviors, or deliberately influences others to practice them, has consciously or unconsciously set themselves against all that is good in the Universe. This can only lead to suffering.

- **Willful Ignorance.** Perhaps the most common malady of humanity is to intentionally and stubbornly maintain ignorance. We will deny responsibility for our actions. We will strive and struggle and beat our heads against a wall, never pausing to consider if there is a better way. We will run away from every truth our heart tries to teach us. We will endlessly repeat the same mistakes and injuries, and insist that nothing is wrong. We will submit to every whim and impulse and never question why. We will forget completely who we are, and pile thick layers of hateful mud around the pleading cries of our own soul. We will expend all our energies in distraction and never relax into the present moment. There are many different circumstances and conditions that lead to this state, but the most common seems to be a strong attachment to pain, self-punishment and despair (the natural results of willful ignorance) because we have not learned compassion for ourselves or understood our purpose in this life.

- **Animalism.** By this I mean a mistaken belief in the supremacy (as opposed to balanced integration) of the Animal[7] in human beings. That is, that the most basic and self-serving of impulses should be celebrated and satisfied above any other, regardless of the cost to ourselves or the well-being of those around us. For most, this attachment to insatiable desire is part of an initial stage of being; it is a natural part of our early development. And so we must have compassion for ourselves and for others who face the constant pull of primitive impulses. But much harm has come into the world through animalists who, even though they are cognizant of the destructiveness of their behavior, have no desire or intention to transcend it. Thus, although all animalists victimize themselves, they are usually eager to draw others down with them in order to validate wanton pleasure-seeking. Evidence of animalism are responses

---

[7] See **Pyramid of Self** in Appendix

like greed, self-serving ambition, covetousness, selfishness, uncontrollable lust, jealousy, destructive anger, aggressive competitiveness, inability to manage thoughtless impetus, and an unabashed and loveless abandonment to the most primal aspects of Self.

- **Invalidation.** Invalidators try to make other people wrong. This has many different forms, the more subtle of which are perhaps the most damaging. Invalidation attempts to undermine spiritual evolution by trivializing, criticizing, teasing, or otherwise harassing and controlling anyone who seeks a healthier and higher Self. The invalidator's (often unconscious) objective is to interrupt further spiritual progress – or better yet, to lure someone into a previous stage of being. Just as an injured or trapped animal may gnaw at its own leg and lash out at others who try to help it, so too invalidators are likely acting from deep hurt or despair, and irrationally justify – or are willfully unaware of – the damage they are wreaking on themselves and others. Behind a false and defensive confidence, invalidators often ridicule and despise themselves even as they seek to dominate, control and tear other people down.

- **Deceptive Manipulation.** *Like a madman who throws firebrands, arrows and death, so is the man who deceives his neighbor, and says, "Was I not joking?"* Deceptive manipulation hates the truth, seeking to confuse what is spiritually healthy with what is spiritually unhealthy. A façade of charismatic and popular facts may paint a persuasive but incomplete picture, encouraging victims to march enthusiastically to their own destruction – or in useless circles. Like invalidation, at the heart of this futility we find fear, self-loathing and lust for control. Frequently the byproduct of a deeper psychological pathology, such behavior can be compulsive, deliberate or both.

- **Legalism.** When malevolent intent is transparent, it is easiest to identify and transform. But it is more difficult to recognize when hidden beneath apparent conformance and propriety, or within actions that seem easily defended as being "within the law" or "in the best interest of all," yet clearly lacking in any real empathy or compassion. This outward conformance to what is superficially right is the core of legalism. Legalism has reared its self-righteous head in nearly every spiritual tradition in human history. At some point, the laudable intentions of a tradition's values are corrupted into inflexible regulations and restrictive edicts, primarily so that a select few in an artificial hierarchy can have power over others. For that is what legalism is all about: creating and maintaining power. Once again, this doesn't define those unwittingly trapped in a rigid system of social, religious or political rules as "evil," but anyone who is conscious of a systemic compulsion to subjugate others, and happily operates within the corrupt falsehood of legalism, will certainly smother the Divine Spark within.

- **Empty Habit.** Very subtle and easy to fall into, empty habit excises all value and joy from spiritual practice, and eventually from life itself. There are contemplative states in which the goal is detachment, and this can be very constructive as a conscious objective. But when we detach from life because we have forgotten our purpose, become emotionally shut down through inattentiveness, or withdraw into ourselves because we have been wounded in some way, we create empty habits. This is why constant renewal and mindful practice are so important: to pay attention to what we are doing and why, every day and with every breath, and to resist complacency and laziness in our self-awareness. Sometimes, when we have fallen out of love-consciousness, the momentum and structure of our spiritual practice may still continue – even as we doubt there was ever any love in us or the Universe. At the darkest depths of empty habit, it might even appear that the power of our beliefs is but fantasy and delusion. Yet if such moments can be transformed into advanced contemplative states, we can begin again from the void of not-knowing, waiting with patience for renewed Light to shine out from our soul, and new meaning to blossom in our hearts.

How do we respond to evil? The great spiritual teachers tell us with patience and genuine compassion. After all, another soul buried under layers of pain and illusion is no different than our own. But the shape and timing of appropriate action must be sought through careful reflection and spiritual discernment, and is always a matter of courage balanced with modesty. When there is no guile in us, when our convictions are formed by Universal objectives, and when our sincere intent is not to injure or malign anyone but to restore people to themselves, then we will naturally expose spiritual antagonists for what they are. Even then, the Light we cast around us does not accuse or attack with bilious fervor; it lifts up wisdom and an unpretentious example of evolutionary being, gently warns of unheeded consequences, and then lets go. For why would a mystic be interested in controlling another's decisions? Ultimately, we all must bear the burdens of our past and present choices alone.

Through ongoing mystical practice, we can become filters of positive transformation, humbly healing what is broken instead of striving against it. Sometimes this will be the result of deliberately crafted artifacts of will – our actively blessing and binding those who curse Life or appear to counteract spiritual evolution. At other times positive change will be a natural outgrowth of who and how we are from moment-to-moment, or a long-term result of vigilantly fulfilling our purpose. And sometimes the cause and effect of curative synthesis will be a complete mystery that goes unnoticed or is quickly forgotten. But every step we take down the mystic's way is a choice to amplify Love and Light in the Universe, and every skill, insight or empowerment we embrace in that journey can lend itself to the good of All. Although the effort of creation is more gradual and understated than the suddenness of destruction, this is how injurious influences are in due course overwhelmed by the sublime.

Staying On Track

How can we overcome our resistance to progressing through different stages of being? How can we keep taking one small step after another through a difficult journey of self-transformation? How can we maintain positive expectations? How can we become ever more intimate with the Sacred? How can we avoid the traps of denial and delusion? Our justifications and modes of operation may change over time, but daily mystical practice as guided by the golden intention offers constant support: an ever-expanding love-consciousness, increasing trust in spiritual sensitivities, a clearer view of interdependencies in and around us, and much more. Through disciplines of heart, mind, spirit and will we nourish and sustain our spiritual Self and bless our surroundings, and our sense of contentment, wellness and generosity will continually inspire greater harmony. Through action springing from deeper understanding and connection, we affirm our own transformation. Through letting go of all attachment to such affirmation, we discover an infinite capacity to grow. Through growing in every dimension of our being, we become the object of our intention.

By attempting we become, by becoming we are, by being we cease all attempts to become. Once this evolutionary process is embedded in our consciousness, we are compelled to keep evolving. There will still be hurdles – created by circumstance and our own inattention – which inform our course with ever more humility and letting go. But we need only return to stillness and emptiness for answers. In the meantime, if we concentrate on incremental practice, the ocean will appear just as vast, but our sense of safety and ability to navigate will improve with each dip of the paddle, and the rushing splendor of every crest and trough will lose its foreboding and offer us thrilling joy instead.

Enhancing Discernment

With every choice, a mystic reinforces the quality of their intentions and their hope for positive change. Yet as we mature, what often begins as blissful serendipity increasingly incurs sober responsibility. To know our own soul is a joyful thing, but also a powerful thing demanding humble integrity. Although it is true that a sincere motivation aligns us with the Source of Light and Life, intention alone cannot repair a decision made in willful ignorance of available information, or excuse a careless impulse that results in inadvertent harm. At the onset of our journey, we will be somewhat insulated from our own ineffective stumbling and lingering pride by the momentum of a mystically-informed course. But at some point there will be a transition into spiritual adulthood where we fully embrace personal accountability for every thought, emotion and action. Essentially, it is a time when the Universe seems to expect us to have learned something, and to apply that learning to our day-to-day lives. This is where discernment can aid us.

Recognizing and trusting our discernment comes through practice. At first, we may seek a mentor to help us understand the process, and synchronicity will likely buttress our decisions. But we cannot rely on these externals to guide us forever. An intellectual understanding of discernment will also fail us, because just as with a gnosis of the Absolute, it is only through diligent and multifaceted interior discipline that we encounter *ahas* that illuminate consciousness and encourage our spirit. Discernment is also consistently dynamic; it seldom rests in previous conclusions, but champions nuance, ambiguity and holism. Like all that mysticism embraces, it is elastic, often fleeting, and can only be experienced directly. We could even say that comprehending the exact nature of discernment requires, well...discernment.

Many factors will combine into moments of discerning insight. Here are examples of some critical input streams:

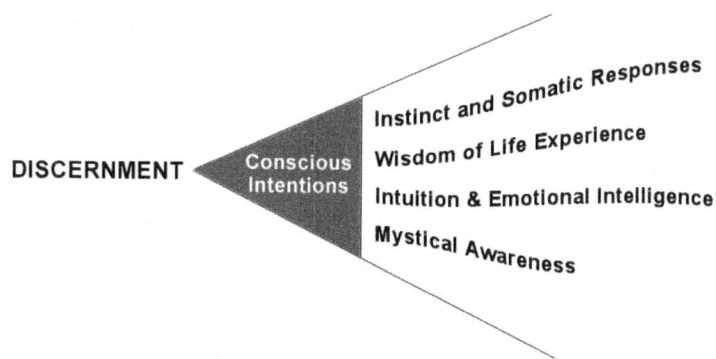

Each input stream requires separate attention and refinement, and although all of them are innate processes, in the modern world there is often little encouragement to nurture them. After all, how often do we really listen to what our bodies are trying to tell us? And the wisdom of our life experience may sometimes contradict what we learn in school or the latest advice from media talk shows. Our intuition may be ridiculed or dismissed by coworkers, family members and sometimes even friends. And mystical awareness will present challenging and paradoxical information, in part because it has a different orientation than other input streams. Where instinct, intuition and experiential wisdom tend to weigh individual choices and concerns of the moment, mystical awareness penetrates Universal trends and eternal consequences. Now consider that all of these may not readily agree with each other – at least not on the surface – and discernment can seem impossible to synergize. However, as we filter each contribution through the golden intention, with sincere confidence that the good of All will be served, our discernment has an anchor and a filter, so that the implications of each choice becomes unquestionably clear.

And once again we come full circle to the heart of the mystic's way: letting go. By releasing our certainty about what is, what our ego demands of us, and even what our past successes have taught us, we invite lucidity and synchronization into current consciousness. By relaxing our dependence on intellect and physical sense, we enter a Sacred inner space where the broadest possible context for our actions is revealed. By letting go of personal attachment to outcomes – and the dominance of any one input stream – disparate information merges into unified insight.

For me, the quickest route to this unification is meditation. Difficult conundrums melt away when the mind is quieted and I am no longer so attached to thoughts and feelings. What swiftly arises is not only distilled vision, but also the underlying principles supporting that vision. Sometimes this can only be explained as an inexplicable "knowing." At other times, in a flash of interconnection, things fit together in ways that make rational sense. And, of course, there is the final necessity of following through. When we support true discernment with action, our wisdom is confirmed and our faith in mystical methodologies deepens. Without follow-through, we may endure the same confirmations, but without the immediate benefit of spiritually healthy outcomes.

6 - THE PROMISE OF HUMAN POTENTIAL

Whether as a species, an amalgamation of cultures, or as part of a global organism, humanity is evolving. As more and more individuals interact with the mystic continuum through disciplined consciousness, the movement of that evolution becomes evermore self-aware. Are we poised on the brink of a major transformation? My intuition tells me that the larger the number of adherents to such a belief, the more likely transformation will occur. Ultimately, it is the choice of the individual to actively contribute to the betterment of the Whole, and a critical mass of positive intention can only enhance pervasive change.

Clearly, one question in every moment is whether or not to exist for a reason. Do we wish to live in harmony with ourselves, each other and the Natural Realm, or promote dissonance, division and destruction? Is a higher order of existence a desirable outcome, or is entropy somehow more attractive? There seem to be implied opposites here, a duality that defies interdependent being or Divine immanence. But this perceived duality is a state of mind. There are only gradations of intention – conformance, resistance and impartiality are but variable gears in the vast mechanisms of the inevitable. If we do not decide for ourselves, there is a high likelihood that our course will be set for us, or that we will be influenced without knowing it. If we do decide how to proceed through life, the ultimate outcome of Unity cannot be thwarted, for it already exists in the past, present and future. What mysticism confirms is that we are all already One, with every individual contributing superlative uniqueness to the Whole. Each of us merely embraces this reality to varying degrees.

As for our personal efforts, the Universe does not tolerate stasis for long, and the energies in and around us constantly excite metamorphosis in everything else. The only meaningful constant is the quality of our consciousness as we engage perpetual change. We cannot always know, but we can become, and mystical awareness leads us to places where the very best of our humanity fully inhabits the now and energizes our spiritual progress. Along the mystic's way, we can choose continuous personal growth as our privilege, unconditional love as our passion, and the good of All as our greatest responsibility. Beyond this lies the freedom of a joyful, creative mystery.

What might a spiritually evolved humanity look like? Or what would happen if there were a decline in cumulative consciousness? Although many mystics and philosophers have tried to answer these questions, an unspecific but probable conclusion is that we will be surprised either way – pleasantly in the case of a deep harmonization of human civilization with the All, unpleasantly in the case of cultural atavism. About the only prediction I would make is that a continued acceleration away from *heart time* and *spirit time* into an increasingly frenetic *head time* will disable soulful self-examination and a balanced approach to life. When we process, evaluate and plan with intellect only, paying undue attention to the loudest and most hurried voices within and without, we cut ourselves off from a more gradual blossoming of holistic wisdom and the gentle whispers of true discernment.

To allow for spiritual growth, I suspect that the engines of material progress need to idle a bit. A continued aggressive adoption of Western-style industrialism, commercialism and consumerism will assuredly retard the evolution of our planet – or perhaps hasten it in ways that undermine human participation. But regardless of our chosen course, there will continue to be plateaus and hurdles for both the individual and the collective. No substantive change can occur without us facing our greatest fears, weaknesses and antagonisms, and even expanded awareness and spiritual acumen will not soften the lessons we must learn in order to mature.

I can imagine a world where there is no illness, no famine, no violence, no poverty, no sorrow...but I can also imagine a world full of even more insanity, destruction and pain than currently exists. Come heaven or hell, my duty is clear: I can either contribute all that I am through the golden intention, or dissipate my energy in egocentric futility. As a mystic I believe that the Universe conspires in favor of my consciousness, and that my consciousness conspires in favor of the Universe. In this way I can joyfully participate in whatever comes, and help transform suffering with love. I am accountable only to myself in this, and the inexorable forces of Life and Light will either include me in the next great stage of being, or discard this manifestation as an inadaptable relic. For now, I can only hope to be a primitive iteration on its way to perfection, and trust that the briefest glimpses of all-inclusive harmony are a promise of things to come.

Different Perspectives on Human Potential

"...To go beyond thought and time – which means going beyond sorrow – is to be aware that there is a different dimension called love. But you don't know how to come to this extraordinary fount, so what do you do? If you don't know what to do, you do nothing, don't you? Absolutely nothing. Then inwardly you are completely silent. Do you understand what that means? It means that you are not seeking, not wanting, not pursuing; there is no center at all. Then there is love."

– J. Krishnamurti

"Love is patient, love is kind, love is not jealous. Love does not brag and is not arrogant. It always acts appropriately, and does not pursue things for selfish advantage. Love is not easily provoked, nor does it dwell on any wrongs it has suffered. It does not take pleasure in the wickedness of others, but rejoices in a life of truth.

Essential Mysticism

Love endures all things, is continually trusting, never ceases to hope, and endures anything. Love never fails."

— The Apostle Paul

"With courage, vision, humor, and creativity, we can use our magic, our ability to change our consciousness, our world view, and our values to reinstate the living web of all interconnected life as the measure by which all choices are judged."

— Starhawk

"A friend once commented, 'Any fool can see that we are in a global ecological crisis. The question is, how do we make a fool care.' We make a fool care by encouraging the wise one to come forth. The wise one already cares. All that is required is that we honor and live by that shining wisdom which, despite our foolishness, passionately exists within us."

— Catherine Ingram

"The problem of thought therefore is to find out the right idea and the right way of harmony; to restate the ancient and eternal spiritual truth of the Self so that it shall re-embrace, permeate, dominate, transfigure the mental and physical life; to develop the most profound and vital methods of psychological self-discipline and self-development so that the mental and psychical life of man may express the spiritual life through the utmost possible expansion of its own richness, power and complexity; and to seek for the means and motives by which external life, society and institutions may remold themselves progressively in the truth of the spirit and develop towards the utmost possible harmony of individual freedom and social unity."

— Sri Aurobindo

"But surrendering to what? It really does not matter what we call it: God or the Tao or the Dharma or the Buddha or our true nature. They are all concepts anyway. It is the act of letting go, of surrendering, that matters. The very act of letting go opens us up completely."

— Dennis Genpo Merzel

"When we live in the dream of the planet, it is as if we are dead. Whoever survives the initiation of the dead receives the most wonderful gift: the resurrection. To receive the resurrection is to arise from the dead, to be alive, to be ourselves again. The resurrection is to be like a child – to be wild and free, but with a difference. The difference is that we have freedom with wisdom instead of innocence."

– Don Miguel Ruiz

"Come to my door at any hour, even if your eyes are frightened by my light. My heart and arms are open and need no rest – they will always welcome you. Come in, my dear, from that harsh world that has rained elements of stone upon your tender face. Every soul should receive a toast from us for bravery! Bring all the bottles of wine you own to this divine table – the earth we share."

– Hafiz (Daniel Ladinsky)

"Merely situate yourself in nonaction, and things will evolve of themselves. Slough off your bodily form, dim your intelligence. Forget all relationships and things; join in the great commonality of boundlessness. Release your mind, free your spirit; be impassively soulless. The myriad things abound, yet each returns to its roots."

– Chuang Tzu (Victor H. Mair)

"Whoever with the devout intensity of their spirit is able to raise the Holy Spark from stone to plant, from plant to animal and from animal to speaking being will lead it to freedom. No setting free of captives is greater than this."

– Baal Shem Tov

"God's joy moves from unmarked box to unmarked box, from cell to cell. As rainwater, down into flowerbed. As roses, up from ground. Now it looks like a plate of rice and fish, now a cliff covered with vines, now a horse being saddled. It hides within these, till one day it cracks them open."

– Jelaluddin Rumi (Coleman Barks)

"To be a mystic is simply to participate here and now in that real and eternal life; in the fullest, deepest sense which is possible to man. It is to share, as a free and conscious agent – not as a servant, but as a son – in the joyous travail of the Universe: its mighty onward sweep through pain and glory towards its home in God."
– Evelyn Underhill

"If you do not know yourselves, then you live in poverty, and you are the poverty."
– *Gospel of Thomas*

"I am the seed that can be found in every creature...for without me nothing can exist, neither animate nor inanimate. But there is no end to my divine attributes...these I have mentioned are only a few. Wherever you find strength or beauty or spiritual power you may be sure that these have sprung from a spark of my essence. But of what use is it for you to know all this...? Just remember that I am, and that I support the entire cosmos with only a fragment of my being."
– *Bhagavad Gita* (Eknath Easwaran)

Concept Affinity: Love-Consciousness

Zen Buddhism	Christian Mysticism	Kabbalah	Sufism	Taoism	Kundalini Yoga
Maitri (Metta) & Karuna	Agape	Chesed Gevurah Tiferet	'Ishq & Mahabba	(Tsyh) Ci	Karuna & Prema

7 - RECURRING QUESTIONS

The following are some questions that seem to surface again and again in my internal and communal mystical discourse. They can be used as starting points for mystical inquiry, the subject of meditation or group discussion, or reminders of the many facets of truth that reveal themselves as we explore the Infinite.

1. What distinguishes mystical experience from other types of experience?

2. Are all mystical experiences spiritual?

3. What are some of the key objectives of mysticism?

4. What are the benefits of escaping habitual modes of thought, action or emotional reaction?

5. What advantages and growth have you experienced through personal discipline?

6. What moments in your life have challenged your assumptions about *what really is* or how the Universe works?

7. What past life events have revealed that you hadn't yet realized something important about yourself?

8. Is returning to a state of emptiness a value judgment of the Universe, a suspension of value judgment, or something else?

9. Where do our fears originate and in what way does mystical practice help us overcome them?

10. From what do you derive your greatest satisfaction and contentment?

11. How can we come to trust any new way of seeing?

12. If you have a highly developed sense of intuition, but the consequences of your actions in response to that intuition seem equally divided between positive and negative results, what might that indicate about your intentions, self-awareness, or self-esteem?

13. How is mystical awareness different from intuition?

14. Why is the golden intention so important to the mystical process?

15. Can you separate the spiritually healthy emotional states you have felt over the past week from the spiritually unhealthy ones?

16. How can we transform malevolent or counterproductive intentions in ourselves and others?

17. Is it possible to cultivate a life that is entirely free of any kind of evil?

18. What does "living in nonduality" look like?

19. What is the role of gratitude in our spiritual evolution?

20. What is "wishing without wanting?"

21. What is the difference between "letting go of ego" and annihilating our own will?

22. Do you believe the same action by the same person, but with different motives, can potentially have different outcomes? Why or why not?

23. What is the difference between being "active" and "passive" for a mystic? What might "doing without doing" mean?

24. What are some characteristics of the transformation of identity that occurs through mystical practice?

25. How have you defined success for yourself? What choices in your life have brought you closer to that success?

26. Do your most important relationships support and contribute to the purpose you have chosen for your life?

27. What are some of the qualitative differences between isolation, loneliness, and constructive solitude?

28. What are some of the differences between common sense and spiritual discernment?

29. What role might mystical practice play in ongoing physical health and emotional healing?

30. What are some other holistic benefits of mysticism?

31. What is compassion?

32. What is wisdom?

33. What is a good guideline for evaluating personal goals and expectations in mystical practice?

34. Why is it imperative to have supportive disciplines in place before activating radical consciousness?

35. What is the single most important feature of all insight?

APPENDIX

The Pyramid of Self

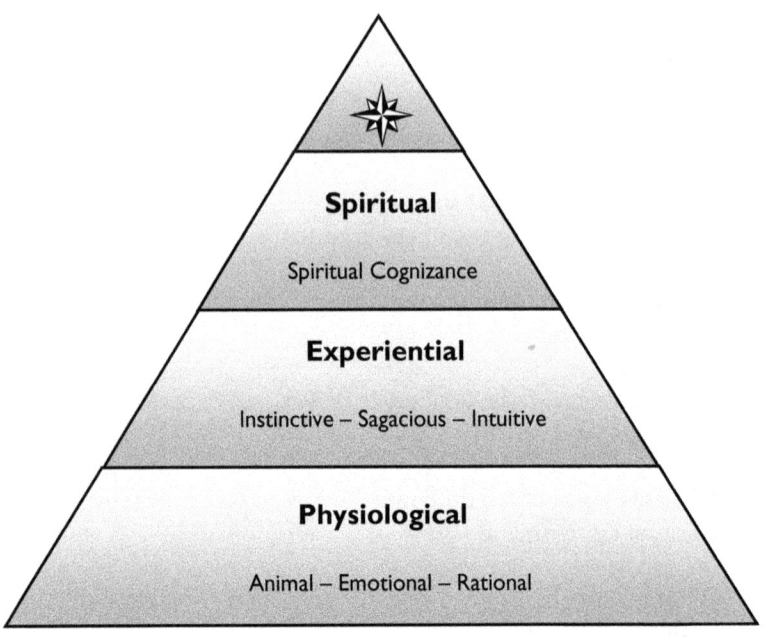

PHYSIOLOGICAL – This is our material being – the basic biochemical creature – and the simplest definition of Self. This can be further broken down into:

> **Animal** – The basic physical requirements for sustaining life and the primal impulses to fulfill them. Hunger, thirst, fatigue, sex drive, aggressiveness, and competitiveness make up the Animal. These are unthinkingly reactive.
>
> **Emotional** – Dominated by basic emotions such as fear, excitement, attachment, anger, greed, guilt, and other emotional preservation impulses. Though initially raw and reactive, these become more constrained, complex and subtle as

we mature. The Emotional also competes with the Rational, introducing complexities in self-awareness and other-awareness – a grayness that contradicts the Rational's preference to see only in black-and-white. The potential synergy between these two is the beginning of a more sophisticated perception and understanding of Self and the world.

> **Rational** – Basic black-and-white logic. A simple comprehension of actions and consequences, observing transparent patterns and relationships, and applying linear problem-solving. The Rational is bent on fulfilling Animal impulses and requirements and is still very attached to our most primitive needs. The Rational also assigns meaning to things. It desires reasons for its own existence and tends to embrace absolutes, especially where right and wrong are concerned. As the Rational advances, however, it begins to challenge these assumptions. In order to resolve such questions, an inherent tension with the Emotional prods us to evolve.

EXPERIENTIAL – This is the information we gather through living and exploring our environment. From our experience, we learn to define ourselves in relationship to others and the world and create boundaries for our will. This level of the pyramid has these components:

> **Instinctive** – The reflexive reactions of fundamental Experiential conditioning and innate somatic knowledge, such as seeking higher ground when lost, running away from a burning building, seeking help when in pain, and following the crowd. One could argue that some of these are genetically programmed behaviors, but even so, without reinforcement through our experience, we would stop responding to them. However, the Physiological still has influence through these instinctive "rules of engagement" with our existence.

> **Sagacious** – Here we begin to have wisdom through observation of our experience, and a more complex, comparative reasoning takes place. Abstract correlations and patterns begin to appear, and the insights we assemble tend to

override more primal, Physiological impulses in our decision-making. Self-control becomes easier and our self-awareness expands. We appreciate understated distinctions, departing from black-and-white logic to embrace larger, less rigid concepts such as patience, tolerance, and exceptions to rules. We become more comfortable with irresolvable contradictions. "Right" and "wrong" are no longer such extreme absolutes. We realize that we don't – and perhaps can't – know anything with certainty. Strict deduction therefore begins to be complimented by Intuitive insight and spiritual discernment.

Intuitive – Something subtle and multifaceted emerges in the Intuitive. We comprehend truths that aren't necessarily logical, but which seem "right" against the backdrop of accumulated knowledge of our life experience and the innate wisdom of our soul. Although these insights are similar to Emotional reasoning, they draw from a deeper sense of *spiritual* preservation and a broader awareness of life's dynamics. Instead of raw fear, there is practical forewarning. Instead of anger, there is sadness and acceptance. Instead of trying to control, we are inspired toward love and compassion, increasing our empathy and awareness of others. In the Intuitive, the seeds of the Spiritual Self and mystical awareness take root and the lush environs of creativity are established.

SPIRITUAL – This is the purely mystical element of Self with which we come to know the Sacred, intensely connecting with our own soul, with spiritual intelligence and with the collective energy of all life. The Spiritual is made up of three forms of spiritual cognizance:

Shared Understanding – The knowledge common to all souls – the instinct of the spirit, if you will – and a window into the nature of our existence. Here we comprehend more deeply that selflessness and discipline are the foundation for building a spiritual life, and that spiritual objectives are a worthwhile pursuit. We also perceive the temporal, impermanent nature of Physiological needs and wants, and embrace kindness, empathy and compassion above all other measurements of morality.

Shared Understanding has no ego, no reactively defensive sense of Self, and thrives on the interconnectedness of all things. Here we differentiate between the Physiologically/Experientially defined Self, and our Spiritual nature. Shared Understanding does not discriminate between *Self* and *Other*.

Moments of Epiphany – Here we make great leaps of comprehension, and our realizations carry with them a powerful emotional, intellectual and spiritual certainty. Such epiphanies may occur in a dream, or as we view a valley from a mountain top, or fall in love, or lose our closest friend, or pray, or meditate, or struggle through a deep depression. Although simple intellectual leaps of understanding can sometimes be predicted or engineered – as when solving a problem or puzzle, for instance – achieving spiritual epiphanies is less formulaic. Our most reliable route is to develop a rich inner life, a life of spirit, which is receptive to such moments and their meaning. These events are so removed from all other aspects of our experience that we know what they are without knowing what they are. Some call them revelations, or prophetic visions, or inspiration, or illumination, and often they seem to strip away all of our previous assumptions. When we choose to listen to our epiphanies and allow them to shape us, these moments powerfully inform and advance our evolution.

Mystical Awareness – The Sufis call this "tasting" the Divine. Mystical Awareness is as solid a sense of the spiritual world as taste, smell or hearing is of the physical world. This is where we directly apprehend underlying realities and mature the wisdom of our souls. Someone in the throes of existential angst might touch on this level of perception-cognition, as might someone lost in meditative concentration, or someone following the promptings of their spirit without fear, or someone who is overwhelmed by a powerful Epiphany. Anyone can access Mystical Awareness, and the long-established disciplines of various spiritual traditions greatly assist our cultivating this faculty. What is most noticeable about this facet of Self is its detachment from both our Physiological and Experiential makeup, and its growing identification – and intimate union –

with the Source of All. This is where spiritual discernment is perfected, our most essential life lessons are processed, and our sense of purpose and completion is achieved. Living in balance with a fully realized Mystical Awareness is also described as a "harmonized existence," in equilibrium with the All. That is, when we have fully understood and successfully integrated spiritual cognizance with our many other aspects of Self, directing those aspects consciously and in concert with each other while continually nourishing and nurturing All Things...then our existence is truly harmonized.

What awaits us at the apex of our pyramid? The Divine Spark, the True Self, the Self in All, the very essence of our soul, and the bedrock of personal reality. Seen by some traditions as the primary objective of mystical practice, and by others as milestone inherent to pursuing what they consider loftier goals, our True Self is both the source and culmination of all other levels of development and experience.

Artifacts of Will

Here is a proposed inventory of what our will can manifest into being at any moment. Whether through action or idea, consciously or unconsciously, these are the ordinary or extraordinary consequences of our intentions.

1. **Meditative neutrality** – Such as returning to emptiness, the art of suspension or equivalent stillness.
2. **Projection of goodwill on others** – Such as trust, compassion, love or encouragement.
3. **Invitation of another's goodwill to Self** – What politicians, managers, and salespeople often try to do.
4. **Supplication for direction of will** – As with prayerful supplication, or seeking guidance from others, or contemplative inquiry.
5. **Subjugation to another's will** – As we do when falling in love, or devoting ourselves to a religious or sociopolitical cause, or as we

might have done as children when we followed our parents or older siblings around like enamored ducklings.

6. **Annihilation of our will** – Such as when we alter our brain chemistry with drugs and alcohol, try to commit suicide, or otherwise permit ourselves to be abused and victimized by external influences.
7. **Integration of another's will and our will** – As with marriage, or a business contract, or playing team sports, or other agreement where there is an assumption of equal participation and investment.
8. **Protecting our will from another's will** – As we do when we withdraw into isolation, or summon the protection of our spiritual tradition, or decline a persuasive request.
9. **Transmutation of another's will** – When we calm aggression, or introduce harmony where there was chaos, or encourage healthy thinking and conduct – without actually imposing our will on someone else. That is, we are welcoming another's will and transforming it. This is often used by skilled counselors, mediators and leaders.
10. **Redirection/Deflection of another's will** – The outcome may be similar to artifacts 2, 8 and 9, and this may have a defensive or corrective intent, where the object of our will may be completely unaware of our influence as the course of their desire is redirected.
11. **Subtraction/Restriction of another's will** – As with physically confining someone, psychologically or emotionally oppressing them, disabling or injuring them in some way, or taking their life.
12. **Enhancement/Expansion of another's will** – This is what is happening when we consciously align ourselves with the good of All, or throw our support behind a leader we believe in, or nurture and nourish someone, or procreate.
13. **Creation of Residual will** – In inanimate objects. I suggest that this has – depending on the intensity, intentions and focus of its creative agent – a specific half-life. In the case of an Immortal Creator, this raises some interesting questions.
14. **Cascading Propagation of will** – As in mass media, group lectures, political rallies, etc. where intentions and ideas spread throughout large numbers of people via intermediaries. An intriguing theory that describes this process is *memetics*.

Mystic Activators Comparison

√ Primary Emphasis • Secondary Emphasis ▽ Incidental (Note: With most of these descriptions, the many subtle differentiations, subsets of practice, or schools for a given category have not been listed separately in this chart.)	The Perfection of Love	Ecstatic Induction	Symbolic & Synchronistic Ritual	Subtractive Meditation
Sufi muraqaba (watchfulness)	•			√
Buddhist zazen (sitting meditation), vipassana (insight meditation/bare attention), and jhana (concentration meditation)	•	▽		√
Bhakti Yoga	√	√	•	•
Kabbalist kavannah (holy intention/concentration)	•	▽	√	√
Christian theoria/contemplatio (contemplative prayer)	√	▽	√	•
Buddhist metta bhavana (loving kindness meditation)	√	▽		•
Gyana (jnana) Yoga	▽		•	√
Hermetic visualization and meditation		▽	√	√
Transcendental Meditation	▽	•	•	√
Other mantra or mandala meditation/Yoga	▽	•	•	√
Sufi dhikr ("remembering" God)	√	•	√	•
Hasidic prayer – hislahavus (bursting into flame) and devekus (clinging to God)	√	•	√	▽
Invoking certain "spiritual gifts" in Christianity (tongues, prophecy)	▽	•	√	▽
Kundalani, kriya, or other tantra Yoga	•	√	√	•
Taoist hsiao chou tien (circulation of Chi meditation)	▽	•	•	√
Chanting, breathing and imagery techniques of ecstatic Kabbalah	▽	√	√	•
Shamanic trance	▽	√	√	•
Trance-inducement via controlled breathing, psychedelic drugs or extended fasting	▽	√		•
Sufi "turning" (ecstatic dancing)	√	√	•	•
Hermetic initiations and symbolic rituals		▽	√	▽
Earth-centered ceremonies such as Wiccan rites of power or polarity	•	•	√	▽
Angelic incantations and use of gematria (numerology of the Hebrew alphabet) in the magical Kabbalah		▽	√	
Divination (Tarot, I Ching, Runes, Bibliomancy, etc.)			√	▽
Christian rituals, such as adult baptism, "laying on of hands" by elders and the Eucharist	•	▽	√	
Energetic healing arts such as Reiki	•		√	▽
Spontaneous Communion (an unintentional state inspired by nature, during sex, through music, during extreme crisis or pain, in a dream, etc.)	▽	▽		▽

SUGGESTED READING

Here are some books that explore mystical ideas and approaches to practice, listed in order of progressively difficult conceptual or practical material. I recommend the most current editions, and would offer these additional caveats:
1. Many authors understandably frame their thoughts within a fairly formalized system of assumptions and beliefs.
2. With too few exceptions, the refinement of an explicit and consistent guiding intentionality is generally underemphasized.
3. Purely external guideposts to truth are seldom reliable, and there is no end to persuasively written books. We should each rely on our own discernment to integrate concepts and practices into the journey we call our own.

The Journey Home, Lee Carroll

The Four Agreements, Don Miguel Ruiz

The Miracle of Mindfulness, Tich Nhat Hanh

The Gift, Poems of Hafiz, Daniel Ladinsky

356 Zen, Jean Smith

The Seven Spiritual Laws of Yoga, Deepak Chopra & David Simon

Miraculous Living, Rabbi Shoni Labowitz

The Spiral Dance, Starhawk

The Bhagavad Gita, Eknath Easwaran

The Essential Rumi, Coleman Barks

Lao-Tzu Te-Tao Ching, Robert G. Hendricks

Total Freedom, J. Krishnamurti

The Mind of Light, Sri Aurobindo

One Taste, Ken Wilber

Will and Spirit, Gerald G. May

Trance, From Magic to Technology, Dennis R. Wier

Mysticism, A Study in the Nature and Development of Spiritual Consciousness, Evelyn Underhill

Cognitive Models and Spiritual Maps, Jensine Andresen & Robert Forman

Thank you for spending time with these words.

For more information about mysticism, the complete downloadable text of the *Vital Mystic*, references and resources I have used in my research, and to order more copies of this book, please visit

www.searchforclarity.com

And so the Infinite beckons....

www.ingramcontent.com/pod-product-compliance
Lightning Source LLC
Chambersburg PA
CBHW061455040426
42450CB00007B/1373